# ART SYNECTICS

By Nicholas Roukes

Davis Publications, Inc.
Worcester, Massachusetts

For Diane

Cover: *The False Mirror (Le Faux Miroir)* by René Magritte, 1928, 21 1/4" x 31 7/8" (54 x 80.7 cm.), oil on canvas. Collection, The Museum of Modern Art, New York.

Title Page: *The Castle in the Pyrenees* by René Magritte, 1959, 79" x 59" (200.6 x 133.7 cm), oil on canvas. Courtesy Harry Torczyner, New York.


Davis Publications, Inc.
Worcester, Massachusetts U.S.A.



Printed in the United States of America
ISBN 0-87192-151-0

10 9 8 7

# PREFACE

*The basic task in the creative process is to bring together, in some useful fashion, ideas which are usually remote from each other.*

S.A. Mednick

The term *Synectic* is from the Greek *Synectikós,* which means "bringing forth together" and "bringing different things into unified connection." This is a form of creative thinking that combines imagination and analogical thinking in order to transform commonplace, familiar elements into new and unusual structures. Through various processes of mixing and matching, exciting metaphors and visual analogues are produced. Since Art Synectics involves the process of fusing disparities, it demands a tolerance for ambiguity and for the initial chaos that accompanies the process of mixing highly diversified elements.

Edgar Allan Poe once described himself as "often drifting into unthought-like thoughts that are inclined to undermine and supercede logic" — an insight into the importance of by-passing the logical brain that often tends to curb radical thinking. For "unthought-like thoughts" — synectic thinking — appeal to the integrated brain: to the intuitive intelligence that stems from our emotional and psychological makeup, and to the logical and more rational brain that allows us to "nail down" feelings and perceptions into hard facts and tangible structures.

In his book, *Synectics,* William J.J. Gordon summarizes three fundamental characteristics of synectic theory: (1) creative output increases when people become aware of the psychological processes that control their behavior; (2) the emotional component of creative behavior is more important than the intellectual component, the irrational is more important than the rational; (3) the emotional and irrational components must be understood and utilized as "precision tools" in order to increase creative output.

This book is divided into six chapters: Analogy; Imaging and Transforming; Signals, Signs, and Symbols; Myth and Mythmaking; Ritual, Game, and Performance; and Paradox. Each chapter contains an overview regarding the selected theme, along with exercises, games, and activities for studio or classroom use. The purpose of *Art Synectics* is to encourage creativity in art through experiences that involve unconventional associations of ideas and images. It is the writer's hope that this book can be used as a creative tool for transforming ordinary perceptions into extraordinary, exciting, yet cohesive structures.

A guiding principle in writing *Art Synectics* was taken from the words of Christopher Morley: *"The purpose of a book is to trap the mind into doing its own thinking."*

N.R. Calgary, Alberta, Canada

# ACKNOWLEDGMENTS

The author is grateful to the artists, galleries, and museums that have contributed ideas and materials for the production of this book.

Every effort has been made to trace copyright ownership of the photographs and illustrations used in this production. If, however, there are omissions or errors, the publisher would appreciate knowing of them in order to make corrections for future editions.

Special thanks to Joan Januszowski for typing the manuscript, Coralee Willis for research assistance, Michael McTwigan for editing the manuscript, and to Michael Ballnik and Hignell Printing Ltd. of Winnipeg, Manitoba, for printing and binding services.

As always, an extra special thank you to Julie Roukes for help in proofreading the manuscript, as well as constructive criticism and empathy during the writing of this book.

The author extends a special invitation to his readers to contribute ideas and art projects for consideration in future editions of *Art Synectics.* Address correspondence to Nicholas Roukes, c/o Juniro Arts Publications, 28 Butte Place, N.W., Calgary, AB, T2L 1P2, Canada.

**Untitled** by Lucio del Pezzo, 1978, 27-3/4" x 19-3/4" (70 x 50 cm), serigraph. Courtesy Studio Marconi, Milan,

# CONTENTS

# CHAPTER 1

# ANALOGY

*Poetry is the achievement of the synthesis of hyacinths and biscuits.*

Carl Sandburg

*ANALOGY: (a-nal-o-ji) Gk. Equality of ratios, proportion; an agreement, likeness, or proportion between the relations of things to one another.*

Century Dictionary

In its literal definition, the term *analogy* means "according to ratio." However, in its broader use it implies *any* similarity between things that are otherwise unlike. As artists, we are interested in analogical thinking because it is an effective tool for stimulating the imagination. By making mental comparisons, or analogical links, known relationships between dissimilar elements can be transferred to each other — and a whole new world of insight, thought, and imagery is possible.

Analogies are convenient ways of intuiting or subjectifying knowlege and experience, whether used simply to make comparisons without "trying to prove anything," or in more sophisticated attempts to derive poetic metaphors. Sandburg's famous line, "the fog comes on little cat feet," is an example of analogy used as a poetic device in literature. The painting by Morris Graves, on the other hand, is a visual analogy that equates certain lines and shapes drawn on the canvas with qualities of sound.

**1. Visual analogy:** although radically different in scale and function, an ear of corn, a high rise building, and a contemporary sculpture are found to have common design qualities that link them as visual forms. The sculpture, **Grande Stele**, is by Rivadossi Giuseppe, 102-1/4" x 20-1/4" (259.7 x 52 cm), wood. Courtesy the artist.

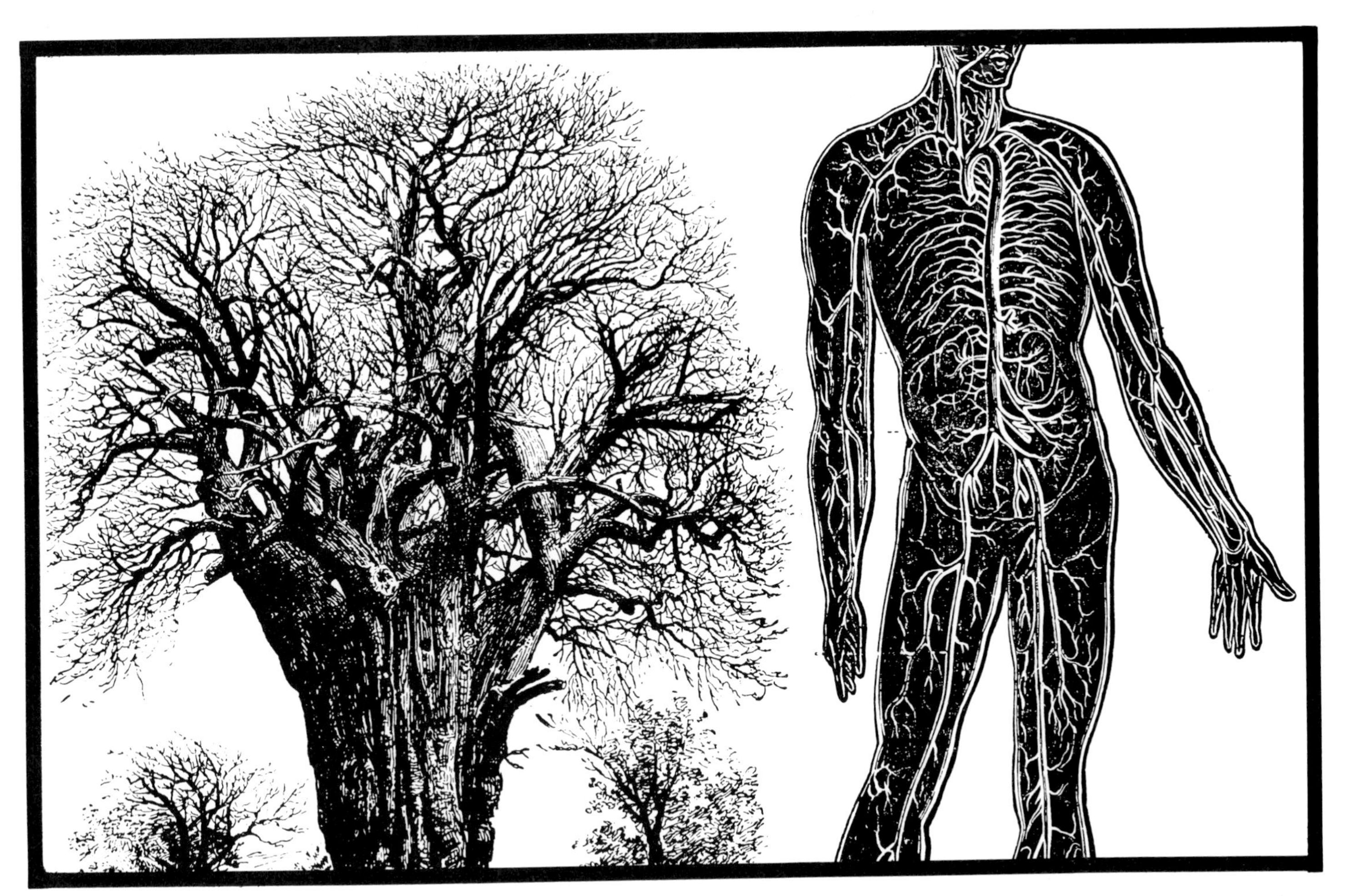

**2. Logical analogy:** the system of a tree is compared to the vascular system of the human body.

## Classifications

Analogies may be classified as either *symbolic* or *nonsymbolic*. Nonsymbolic analogies are simple comparisons of different things that in some way resemble each other, either on a logical, sensory, or emotional level. Symbolic analogies, on the other hand, are *metaphoric* in nature; the properties transferred to each other tend to ignite or spark an insight to a "larger idea." For the sake of discussing and applying analogy to the study of Art Synectics, four basic classes of analogy are presented: (1) logical, (2) affective, (3) synaesthetic, (4) paradoxical.

**Logical Analogies.** Logical analogies infer similarities of design, structure, or function between diverse elements. For example, a duck can be compared to an amphibious boat, the skeleton of a fish to a tree, the meandering pattern on the surface of a coral to a river, and so on.

In seeking structural analogies, the artist might compare the design of a bridge to the structure of the human skull — or to the cross section of a bird's wing. Here the artist is not concerned merely with similar surface appearances, but is seeking similarities in design logic or engineering systems that can be transferred from one subject to another.

Functional analogies compare the working operations of one system to another, as when the human nervous system is compared to the electric wiring system of a radio transmitter and receiver, the propulsion system of a squid to that of a jet aircraft, and so on.

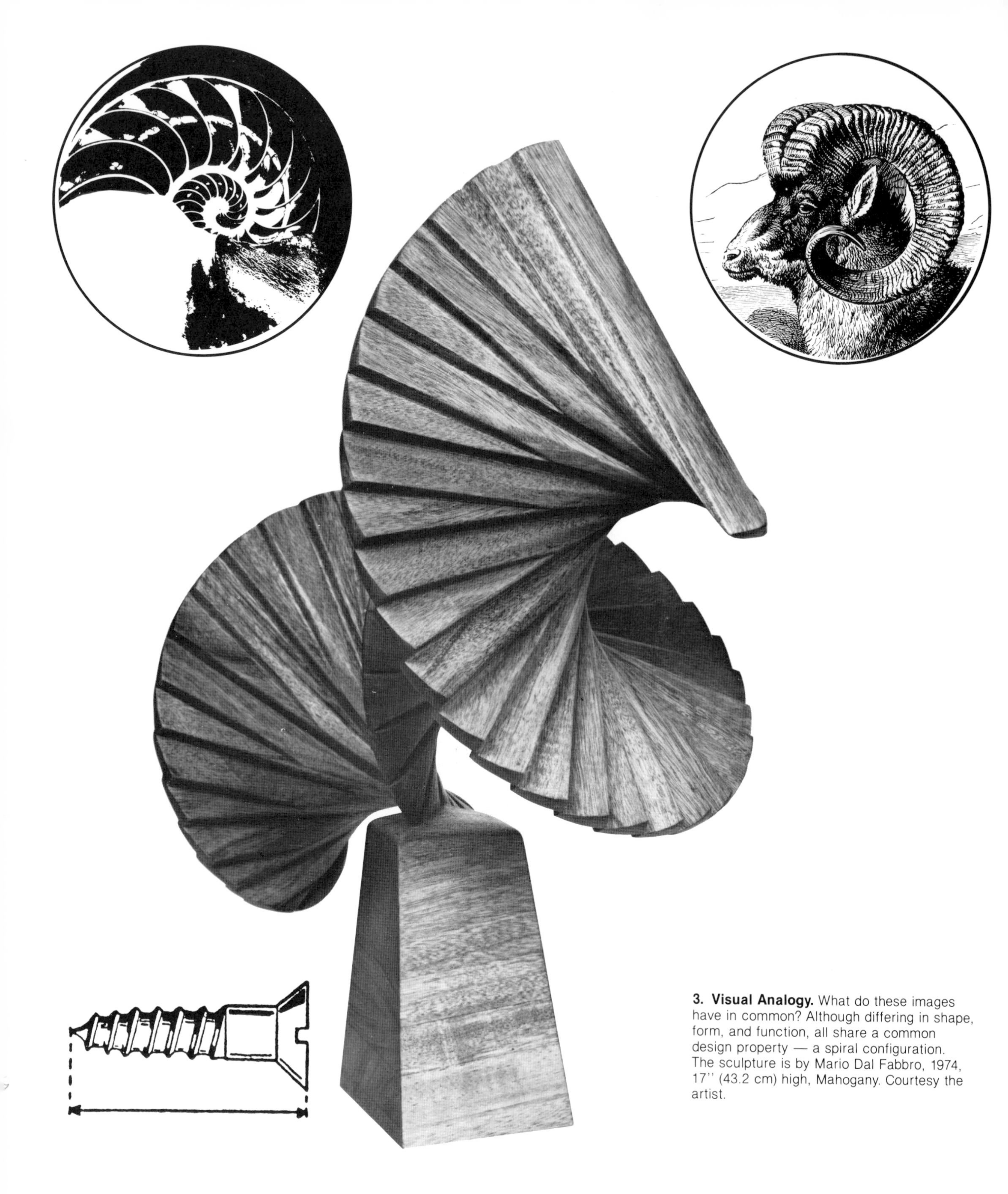

**3. Visual Analogy.** What do these images have in common? Although differing in shape, form, and function, all share a common design property — a spiral configuration. The sculpture is by Mario Dal Fabbro, 1974, 17'' (43.2 cm) high, Mahogany. Courtesy the artist.

**4. Vortex** by Graham Boyd, 1972, acrylic, nylon monofilament, fishing weights. This is a structural analogy of a phenomenon of nature inspired by the observation of swirling masses of water.

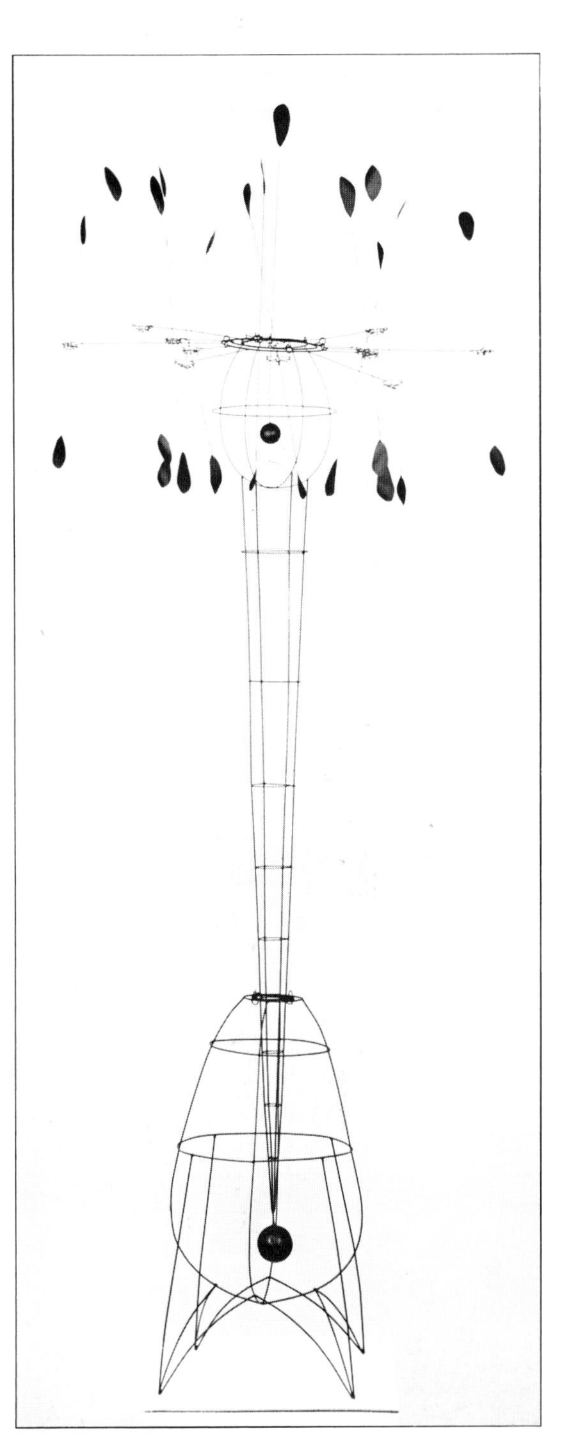

**right: 5. Flower** by Konstantin Milonadis, 38'' (96.5 cm) high, music wire. Courtesy the artist. Inspired by organic growth and form in nature, the artist has created his own visual equivalent of a flower — a finely balanced construction made of steel wire.

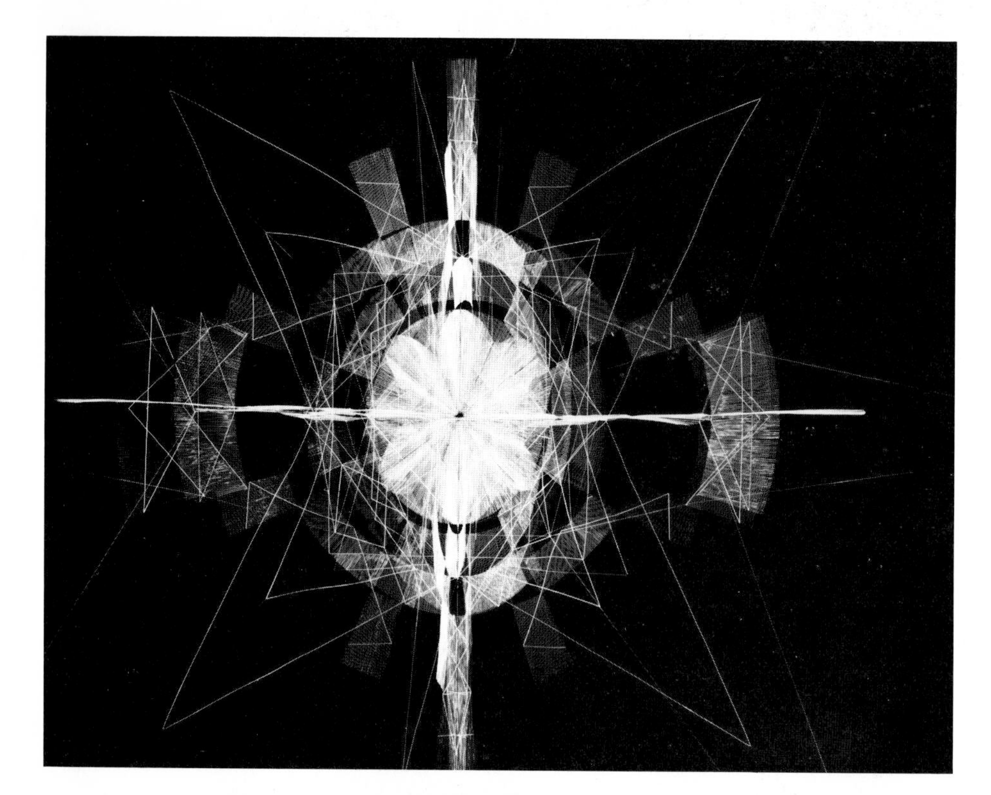

**left: 6. Variations within a Sphere, #10** by Richard Lippold, 1956, 5-1/2' (1.7 m) in diameter, gold-filled wire. Courtesy The Metropolitan Museum of Art, New York. Radiant solar energy is the subject of this skillfully crafted, sculptural analogue.

**below: 7. Birthday** by Marc Chagall, 1915, 31-3/4" x 39-1/4" (80.6 x 99.7 cm), Oil on canvas. Courtesy the Museum of Modern Art, New York. Chagall's work is an example of affective analogy synthesized in a visual form. Drawing more from his personal feelings regarding the subject rather than concern for proportion, the artist takes major liberties in abstracting the elements in his composition.

**8.** Synaesthetic Analogy: **Bird Singing in the Moonlight** by Morris Graves, 1938-39, 26-3/4" x 30" (67.9 x 76.2 cm), gouache. Courtesy Museum of Modern Art, New York. Both abstract and representational images are combined to graphically portray the bird and the "sound" of its music.

**Synaesthetic Analogies.** Synaesthetic analogies are sensory comparisons of an *interdisciplinary* nature: perceptions of touch, sound, vision, taste, or smell can be transferred from one sensory mode to another. For example, in the landscape entitled *Foghorns,* Arthur Dove visualized sound in a graphic form. Musical compositions are often synaesthetic notations of visual, tactile, and/or olfactory perceptions as well.

**Affective Analogies.** Affective analogies are *emotional* resemblances, as when an offensive person is regarded as a snake or a skunk; a beautiful girl as a flower, peach, or honey; an innocent child as a lamb; an aggressive person as a bull or a tiger; a timid person as a mouse, et cetera. Visual images can be *subjectified* through *empathic projection.* When we empathize with someone or something, a strong personal identification is established with the subject. The empathizer projects special feelings and emotions into the subject, whether the subject be another person or living thing, or even an inanimate object such as a rock.

Many scientists and inventors have made major discoveries through empathic projection. The inventor T.A. Rich, for example, once imagined himself to be an electron in order to solve a technical problem. By attempting to "behave" like an electron, he gained the required insight to solve the problem that eluded him. It has been said that Albert Einstein developed his theory of relativity as a result of empathic projection: Imagining himself as a rider of a beam of light, he asked, "What would the world be like from this point of view?" In relation to art, Kandinsky's statement that "everything has a secret soul" may have prompted Jung's explanation that artists "often psychologically project part of their psyches into objects, thus allowing for their animation."

**Paradoxical Analogies.** In daily conversation, we often use paradoxical phrases or figures of speech: "loud silence," "the living dead", "organized confusion." In literature or art, certain combinations of words or images may also seem illogical or contradictory, but upon reflection we discover them to be well-founded. They may also be powerful metaphors in their symbolic meaning as well. Such is the case with the surreal analogies of Salvador Dali. Dali coined the term "paranoic analogy" to describe delusions he likened to dream imagery. In his early paintings, for example, we find images of heads propped up by crutches in strange landscapes. To Dali these paintings were "paranoic analogies of sleep," wherein sleep was conceived to be a state of equilibrium, or even a monster, into which bodies disappeared; only the head remained, supported by crutches. Such illogical combinations of images evoke powerful emotional responses; our minds tell us no logical reason exists for these images to be together, yet since they *are* together and cannot be dismissed from our consciousness, we are forced to reconcile them through the logic of our emotions.

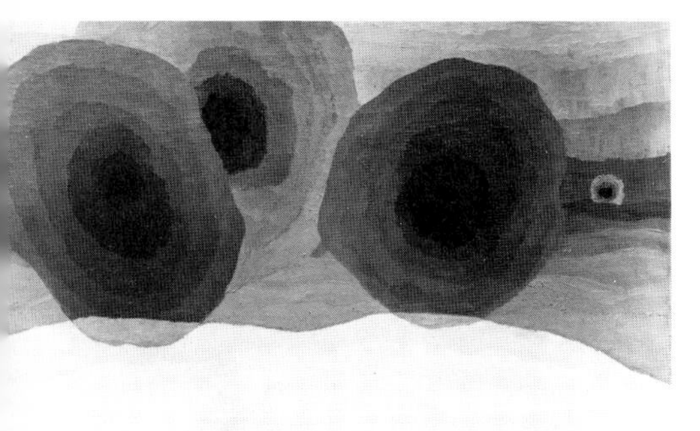

**9. Fog Horns** by Arthur G. Dove, 1929, 17-3/4" x 25-1/2" (45.1 x 64.8 cm), oil on canvas. Courtesy Colorado Springs Fine Arts Center. The artist applies synaesthetic transfer to sensory perception and expression in order to represent sounds in graphic form.

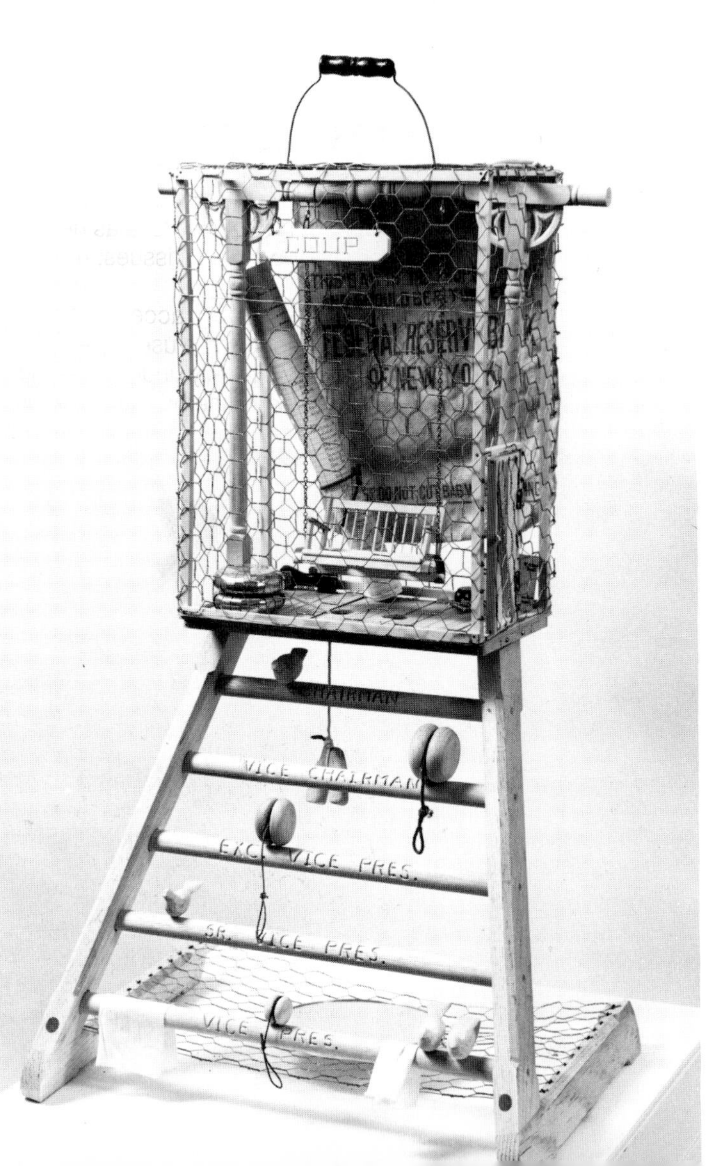


**right: 10.** Paradoxical Analogy: **Climbing the Success Ladder** by Tommy Simpson, 1976, 45" x 24" (114.3 x 61 cm), wood, wire, metal. Courtesy the artist. The artist selects a cage-like structure combined with a step ladder to invectively portray the plight of the ambitious business executive.

## Riddles and Puns

Riddles are humorous analogical puzzles that require ingenuity for their solution. They feed upon paradoxical comparisons and often rely on clever word play for their explanations. Example: *Why do some officers of the law wear patterned suits? For routine checks.* Puns are created by the humorous use of words (word play) and capitalize on words that sound alike, or nearly alike, in order to produce odd or ludicrous ideas. Example: *How can you tell a city dude in the country? He's the one who shoots from the lip.* Words that sound alike yet have highly different meanings are creative tools for cartoonists and artists as well as writers. To motivate the imagination, try making up a list of riddles that have no answers. For example, how many responses can you think of for the following riddles: *Where do you look for a lost cloud? What did the bicycle say to the doctor? Why did the spider kiss the duck? Why do they put jelly beans in transistor radios?*

## Metaphor

Metaphor is the symbolic extension of analogy. Suzanne Langer describes a metaphor as an *idea* expressed by language, which in turn functions as an expressive symbol. A metaphor does not analyze or explain the idea it conveys; instead, it formulates a *new concept* for the imagination. Although metaphors often contain contradictions, they are normally *logical* contradictions with overriding *messages* that transcend their paradoxical structures.

The art of the '80s may well emerge as the decade of personal metaphor. According to Lynda Hartigan, speaking at the 1980 International Sculpture Conference in Washington, D.C., a great number of artists are turning their art inward, using metaphor to explore and define their own identity, tapping such sources as heritage, myths, metaphysics, technology; social, political, and moral issues; dreams, nostalgia, satire, humor, and enigma.

By choosing metaphors carefully, the artist determines how accessible his art is to the viewing public. If very personal or cryptic metaphors are used, the work is hidden to a large degree from public perception. Yet, if universally understood metaphors are combined with private ones, controlled access to the work is allowed.

**11. Reclining Figure** by Henry Moore, 1941, 15" x 22" (38 x 55.9 cm), chalk, pen and ink, watercolor. Collection University of Colorado, Denver. Photo courtesy the artist. By synthesizing the properties of both man and nature in a single work (man is likened to a mountain), the artist symbolizes man's indomitable ability to survive.

**12. The Poetess** by Juan Miró, 1940, 15" x 19-3/8" (38.1 x 48.7 cm), oil on paper. Collection Mr. and Mrs. Ralph F. Colin, New York. Photo: Soichi Sunami. The artist conveys the sensitive qualities of a poet without the use of conventional representational imagery, relying instead on abstract design to create a pictorial analogue.

# Graphic Representation

Artists create graphic images to represent subjects from the real world. All graphic images are *abstractions* that may be classified within three basic types: (1) projections, (2) likenesses, (3) surrogate images.

**Projections.** Projections are "point-to-point" representations of a subject: photographs, shadows, maps, drawings, paintings, and sculptures can be highly accurate representations of the original subject. Trompe l'oeil art, or the super-realistic paintings of William Harnett, fall within this category as well.

**Likenesses.** Likenesses are *stylized* representations of a subject; they can take the form of caricatures, simplified drawings, or any graphic form that is abstracted yet retains recognizable aspects of the original subject.

**Surrogate Images.** Surrogate images are representations of a *symbolic* nature; certain shapes, forms, or marks *stand-in* for the original subject. They are a kind of symbolic shorthand wherein lines and shapes that are entirely different from the original subject are substituted in order to gain symbolic expression. The portrayal of a *cube with wings of wax,* for example, may be said to be a surrogate image of Icarus, the adventurous youth of Greek mythology.

**13. Ceres** by Günter Haese, 1970, 21-1/2" x 9" x 9" (54.5 x 23 x 23 cm). Courtesy Marlborough Gallery, Zurich. A biotic analogue created by analysis and observation of growth forms in nature.

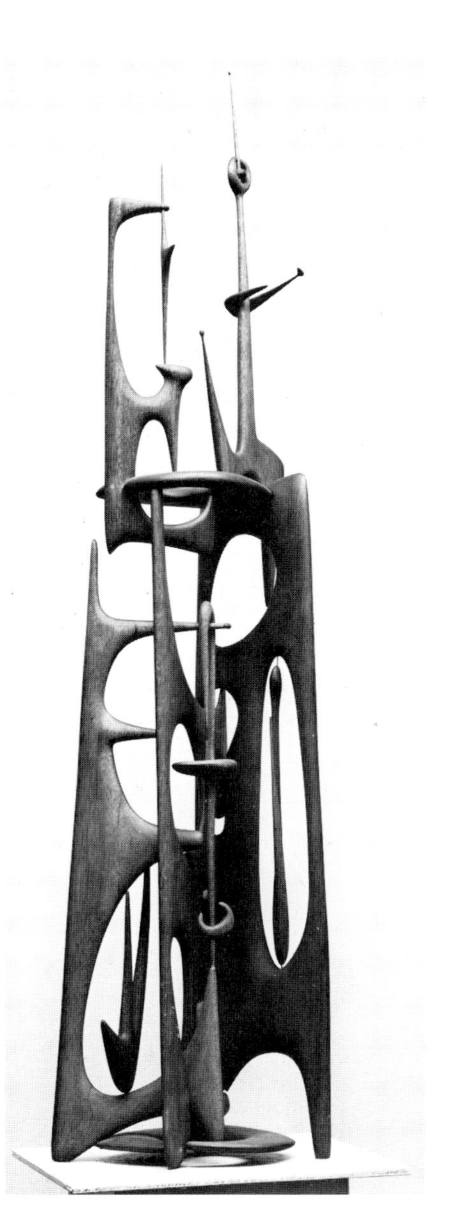

**14. Jungle** by Leo Amino, 1950, 56" x 12" x 11-1/2" (142.2 x 30 x 29.2 cm), Mahogany. Courtesy The Whitney Museum of American Art. Interpenetrating abstract shapes alluding to human-like forms suggest qualities of a claustrophobic "urban jungle."

**15. Lithocireus Magnificus** (model) by Hackel, Glass. Courtesy the American Museum of Natural History, New York.
A radiating growth pattern is observed in this species of Radiolaria.

# 1

# ACTIVITIES

### 1-1 / Analogical Design Systems

**Concept:** Finding design likenesses in dissimilar structures

**Do:** 1. Examine the diagrams in the illustration (right).

2. On a sheet of paper, write down the names of the six systems.

3. Next to each category, write down as many different things you can think of that also belong to each system. For example radiating sytems: wheels, sun, sea star, shower, radio transmitter, family tree, et cetera.

4. Art Activity: Make a collage. Find images that are different, yet related, because of their design properties. Paste them down to form a composition.

5. Add to the list of design systems found in nature. In addition to the spiral, vertebraic, radiating, cluster, branching, and interlocking, what other categories can you think of?

**16. Systems Found in Nature.** A. Spiral, B. Vertebraic, C. Radiating, D. Cluster, E. Branching, F. Grid, G. Interlocking.

## 1-2 / Abstracting Design from Nature

**Concept:** Using nature as a basis for design analysis and transformation.

**Do:** 1. Carefully study the illustrations of radiolaria and diatoms on pages 14 and 15.

2. Make some preliminary sketches based on observations and analysis of these designs. Change, simplify, elaborate, combine, transform the images as you desire.

3. Make a cut-paper design. Cut out the component shapes of a selected drawing, along with shapes and lines to suggest surface decoration, texture, et cetera. Use colored construction paper or colored plastic-surface paper. Paste the components on a black background paper to create an abstract composition.

**below: 17, right: 18. Radiolaria**, a type of marine protozoa (below), and water-borne algae, diatoms, (right). Drawings courtesy Dover Publications (from *Art Forms in Nature* by Ernst Haeckel).
Drawings by Ernst Haeckel, published in *Art Forms in Nature*. New York: Dover Publications, 1974.

**below: 19. A Piece of Pie and a Sandwich Eating Lunch** by Marvin Jones, 24" x 30" (61 x 76.2 cm), hand-colored etching. Courtesy the artist.

**below: 20.** The cartoonist empathizes with an alarm clock and draws it as if it had human qualities.

## 1-3 / Empathic Projection

**Concept:** The imaginative projection of personal feelings into a selected object.

**Do:** 1. Identify emotionally with an object and animate it through empathic projection: Imagine you're a tree, a building, fireplug, porcupine, hammer, rock, et cetera.

2. Write a Haiku poem regarding one of the objects you've imagined yourself to be.

3. Make a drawing or cartoon of that situation.

4. Make a collage incorporating a photograph of yourself along with other collage elements.

## 1-4 / Situations and Similitudes

**Concept:** Developing imagination in perceiving relationships between dissimilarities.

**Do:** 1. Make two lists: one of situations, the second of "stretched" similarities. Example:

| Situations | Similitudes |
|---|---|
| Potatoes frying in oil | Taking final exams |
| Diving off the high board | Exploring new ideas |
| Gluing wood together | Making friends |
| A snow storm | Momentary forgetfulness |
| Water suddenly freezing | Getting a great idea |

Note: There are no wrong answers! Stretch your imagination to make unconventional comparisons.

## 1-5 / Imagine You're an Alarm Clock

**Concept:** Developing skills of imagination and empathic projection.

**Do:** 1. Imagine you're a ________. (Fill in the blank.)

2. Make a cartoon of the character or object you are imagining. Draw a picture or cartoon in the middle of a large sheet of white drawing paper. Add cartoonist's "balloons" around the drawing and print the text that describes your feelings.

**21. The Dancers** by Heinrich Kley, pen and ink. Courtesy Dover publications. Published in *The Drawings of Heinrich Kley.* New York: Dover Publications, 1961.

Can you imagine elephants as ballet dancers? or:
Frogs ice skating?
Bugs as bionic machines?
Spoons as jet airplanes?
Guns as people?
Pencils as artists?
A loaf of bread as a deck of cards?
Shoes as pets?
Bowling pins as skyscrapers?
Clothes acting human without humans in them?

## 1-6 / Paradoxical Analogies

**Concept:** Making "impossible" comparisons

**Do:** 1. Make up a list of paradoxical comparisons such as the list above.

2. Visualize one or more of the situations by making a drawing, cartoon, collage, or three dimensional sculpture.

## 1-7 / Symbolic Thinking

**Concept:** Using analogy as a tool for symbolic thinking.

How is the brain like a boiler?
How is a book like a carriage?
How are words like a bridge?
How is time like an eraser?
How is life like fine crystal?

**Do:** 1. Write out several different responses to the questions above.

2. Make up an additional list of symbolic analogies. Write out responses to each.

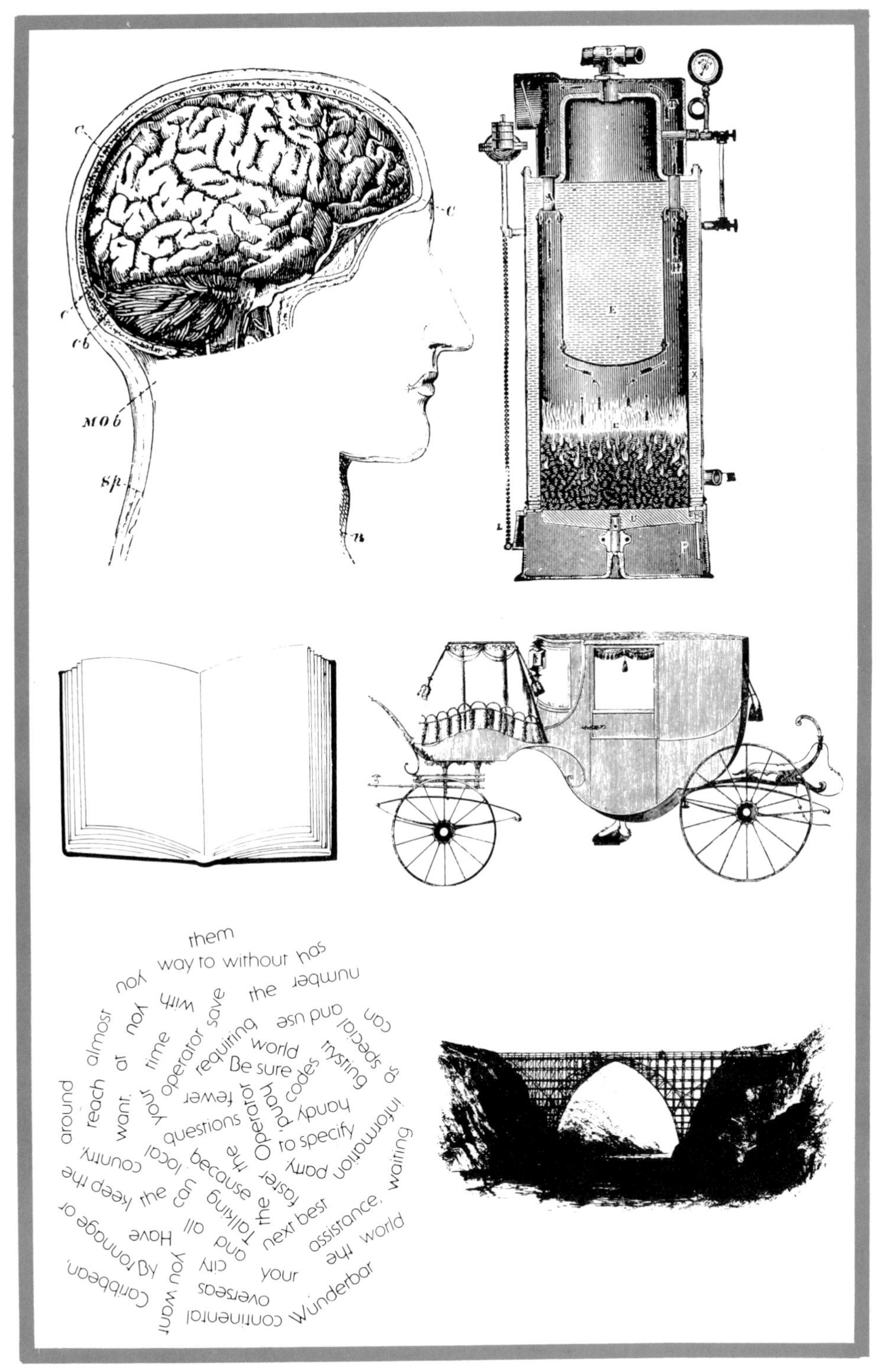

**above: 22. Symbolic Visual Analogy:** How is the brain like a boiler? - How is a book like a carriage? - How are words like a bridge?

23. **Geometric Abstraction: The Laocoon Group** by Tom Brandon, Collage. Courtesy the artist.

## 1-8 / Symbolic Geometrics

**Concept:** Substituting geometric shapes for figurative images.

**Do:** 1. Select a reproduction of a representational art work.

2. Reinterpret the composition, but use only geometric and free form shapes in place of the original shapes and forms. Maintain the composition and proportions of the original work.

## 1-9 / Synaesthetic Analogies

**Concept:** Creating sound-graphic equivalents.

**Do:** 1. Select one of the following themes: (a) jungle noises, (b) marching band, (c) bird sounds, (d) city sounds, (e) carnival, (f) demolition derby, (g) football game, (h) ocean beach.

2. Create a composition that is an abstract equivalent of the selected theme. Do not use pictures or images in this composition; rely only on lines, dots, shapes, forms, textures, colors, et cetera, to portray your ideas.

## 1-10 / Audio-Visual Analogies

**Concept:** Creating sound-graphic equivalents.

**Do:** 1. Record a series of sounds with a tape recorder. Include a variety of sounds such as nonsense sounds (human); sounds from gadgets and devices that are manipulated: tearing paper, crumpling cellophane, tapping objects, spilling water, sandpaper against sandpaper, et cetera; environmental sounds: automobile engines, tennis game, old pumps, street car, fire engine, et cetera.

2. Edit the sounds to produce a three minute tape.

3. Create a visual equivalent of the taped sounds. On a long strip of paper, use lines, shapes, forms, textures, colors, collage, and cut-outs from magazines to make a "graphic time-line."

## 1-11 / Visual Puns

**Concept:** Creating visual puns from words that sound alike, or figures of speech that have double meaning.

**Do:** 1. Make up a list of words or phrases that have double meaning:

| | |
|---|---|
| Strong Box | Fan Club |
| Watch Dog | Pen Pals |
| Fly Paper | Bookworm |
| License Plates | Tow Truck |
| Photo Bug | Watergun |
| Car Pool | Second Hand Store |
| Arms Race | Loud Tie |
| Fingerbowl | Six feet undergound |
| Water Closet | Eggbeater |
| Coat of Arms | Attached to his Dog |
| Bedspring | Sank in His Chair |

2. Mentally visualize a preposterous or outrageous image that stems from these words or phrases.

3. Make a pencil or pen-and-ink drawing from one of your ideas.

4. Make a three-dimensional sculpture in clay or papier-mâché from one of the themes.

More visual puns:

| | |
|---|---|
| Lighthouse | Brain Cell |
| Night Awls | Shoe Tree |
| Backhand | Navel Orange |
| Offspring | Boxing Match |

**24. Mothball** by Patti Warashina, 1976, 30''x18''x15'' (76.2 x 45.7 x 38 cm), handbuilt lowfire clay and underglaze. Courtesy the artist.

**25. Watergun** by Lukman Glasgow, mixed media. Courtesy The Arco Center for Visual Art, Los Angeles.

## 1-12 / Subliminal Messages

**Concept:** Developing awareness towards discovering hidden meanings or implications in commercial advertisements.

Subliminal images and messages are those used in advertising that exist or function outside the area of conscious awareness.

**Do:** 1. Collect advertisements from various newspapers and magazines.

2. Paste each ad on a sheet of large paper, allowing lots of space around each for notes.

3. Circle portions of the ad and extend lines out to the margins. Contemplate the images, the juxtaposition of images, settings, details, et cetera, and write out what the advertisers want you to believe (regardless of what the ad says). Seek out the psychological implications of the ad, the hidden meanings (subliminal messages) and inconsistencies you perceive.

**26.** A "conversation" in design.

## 1-13 / Musigram

**Concept:** Creating an audio-visual analogue.

**Do:** 1. Select a record of either classical, jazz, pop, country, or rock music to interpret.

2. Divide a large sheet of drawing paper with pen or pencil into a number of grids or compartments, corresponding to the number of cuts on the record.

3. Using only lines, shapes, textures, and colors, interpret the music by making a graphic equivalent.

4. Label the composition, along with the title for each cut.

## 1-14 / Speaking in "Design"

**Concept:** Substituting color, form, and texture for text.

**Do:** 1. Cut out images from magazines or newspapers — people, animals, objects, buildings, et cetera.

2. Paste the images on white drawing paper, allowing lots of space around them. Draw cartoonist's "balloons' for each image.

3. Portray a dialogue in "design"; use only lines, textures, and colors (no text).

4. Draw your own characters in cartoon form and have them speak in "design."

## 1-15 / Eccentric Analogies

**Concept:** Developing visual imagery through "forced" comparisons.

**Do:** 1. Make a list of words of things, people, and phenomena.

2. Divide the list into two columns. Example:

| | |
|---|---|
| Rain | Car |
| Boat | Pyramid |
| Earth | Unicorn |
| Door | Beach |
| Brick | Forest |
| City | Frying Pan |
| George Washington | Toothbrush |

3. Arbitrarily (or with the throw of dice) connect words from one column to the other.

4. Contemplate the "forced comparison" and visualize by making a drawing, painting, collage, cartoon, or photograph.

5. Make a three-dimensional visualization of your idea with mixed media: paper, found objects, clay, wood, et cetera.

## 1-16 / Form/Movement Designs

**Concept:** Ordering information into data systems.

**Do:** 1. Make a design that integrates at least two different types of "information." Example:

*Subject: Seagull*

Data:

A. *Form:* shape, color, texture.

B. *Movement:* flight, movement patterns, etc.

2. Visual application: Make a composition that illustrates *10% of A* (form data) and *90% of B* (movement data)

**above right: 27. Unicorn** by Jonathan Meader, 1976, drawing. Courtesy the artist.

**above center: 28. Elephants at a Pub** by Heinrich Kley, pen and ink. Courtesy Dover Publications.

## 1-17 / Anthropomorphics

**Concept:** Imbuing animals, plants, or objects with human qualities.

**Do:** 1. Use clay or pen and ink to depict one of the following situations:

Birds on a coffee break
Elephants at a pub
Pencils jogging
TV's watching TV
Frogs at a disco
Rocks getting married
Cabbages listening to stereo
Corn vs. carrots playing baseball

Add to the list and develop one of the themes with your choice of art materials.

## 1-18 / Interview a Building

**Concept:** Fostering Empathic Projection.

**Do:** 1. Imagine how it would feel to be a particular building in your city. Visit it.

2. Make a line drawing of the building, or photograph it with a camera.

3. Paste the image of the building on a sheet of white drawing paper, allowing space around the image for cartoonist's "balloons."

4. Make up a list of questions to ask the building and print them inside the balloons. Examples:

What's your ancestry? (architectural style)

Are you married? (attached to other buildings)

Are you well organized? (efficiency of interior movement)

Can you see? (inside lighting, windows, obstructions by other buildings)

How do you get along with your friends? (architectural integration)

Can you breathe? (ventilation)

Are you comfortable? (warm/cold air control)

How's your constitution? (plumbing)

How's your nervous system? (electrical wiring)

How's your love life? (tender loving care by owners or tenants)

5. Make a tracing of the original drawing and balloons. In the second drawing, write out the building's responses to the questions (based on your research and observation).

6. Mount the two drawings together.

7. Other themes: Select another architectural object from your environment and make up a list of questions and answers. Interview a factory, bank, hamburger stand, bridge, school building, gas station, bus station, newspaper kiosk, et cetera.

**29.** An "interview" with a building.

CHAPTER 2

# IMAGING AND TRANSFORMING

*The world of reality has its limits; the world of imagination is boundless. Not being able to enlarge the one, let us contract the other.*
Jean Jacques Rousseau

Man's quest for personal identity drives him in two directions: outward, into the existing world of terrestrial reality, and inward, into the subjective world of fantasy and psychic imagination. The ability to produce images is a natural human phenomenon; everyone generates mental images of one sort or another, either of a controlled or autonomous nature.

## What Are Mental Images?

In *The Dictionary of Psychology,* a mental image is defined as "an experience which reproduces or copies in part, and with some degree of sensory realism, a previous perceptual experience in the absence of the original stimulation." Images can be activated through any sense perception — seeing, hearing, touching, tasting, or smelling — and can be grouped into six principal categories: (1) memory images, (2) imaginary images, (3) hypnagogic images, (4) dreams, (5) hallucinations, (6) afterimages.

**left: 30. Swami Vishnu #5** by Robert Moon, 1970, 20-1/2" x 26-1/4" (52 x 66.7 cm), lithograph. Courtesy The Museum of Modern Art, New York. The figure seemingly defies the laws of gravity as it symbolically portrays the transcendental state of mind and the tranquility achieved through the meditative states of hatha yoga.

**right: 31. Portrait of Rudolf II as Vertumnus** by Giuseppe Archimboldo. Courtesy Skokloster Slott, Sweden.

HASTED
VII '76

**Memory Images.** Memory images are retrievals or recollections of past input. They are not the products of fantasy, but are simply straight-forward mental reconstructions of past experience. Our most typical visualization experience is that associated with memory. Interestingly enough, Arthur Schopenhauer defined the madman as a person who "has lost his memory." Without memory as a touchstone to reality and as a day-to-day survival tool, human beings lack a map of previous knowledge to guide them in appraising new sensations and experiences.

**Imaginary Images.** Imaginary images, though based on mental reconstructions of past experiences, are images that are radically *rearranged* by the subconscious. Within this realm of visualization, images are transformed by the artist's fantasy into new mental inventions. Any mental process demanding abstraction or creative thinking relies heavily on the mind's capacity to produce imaginary images.

**Hypnagogic Images.** Hypnagogic images are imaginary experiences usually perceived in the twilight state of consciousness between sleep and waking. In their book, *Seeing with the Mind's Eye,* Mike and Nancy Samuels describe hypnagogic images as reverie images beyond the reach of conscious control, and usually accompanied by various forms of light flashes, sparks, geometric forms, and so on. Although they may seem quite "real" to those who perceive them, hypnagogic images are internal, autonomous images.

**Dreams.** Dreaming is associated with that period of sleep known as the REM (Rapid Eye Movement) cycle, which is the most common generator of vividly perceived images. Each person has between three to five dreams every night, even though they may not be recalled in the wakeful state. Dreams are also internally produced autonomous images, that is, without benefit of conscious control. While dreaming, the mind conjures up strange and paradoxical images, often combining memories along with subconscious desires and anxieties. Here, the laws of space-time continuum are interrupted or reversed: the dreamer may at one moment see himself as an adult, then abruptly as a child, or suddenly as a bird in flight. While in the altered dream state, the dreamer actually believes that what is happening is "real."

**left, opposite page: 32. The Right of Silence** by Michael Hasted 1976, 24" x 20" (61 x 51 cm), oil on canvas. Courtesy the artist. Mysteriously, a typewriter expresses ideas of nature in graphic form — an astonishing departure from its typical function.

**above: 33. Translation** by Al McWilliams, 1975, 13-1/2" x 7-3/8" x 7" (34.3 x 18.7 x 17.8 cm), wood, plastic. Courtesy the artist.

Freud has taught us that dreams, though seemingly irrational, actually do have significant underlying meanings that can be made clear through proper interpretation. In dreams, external perceptions and memories are symbolically altered and integrated into dream images.

Often dreams are sources of answers to special problems, although they may appear in a disguised form. Friedrich August Kekulé, the German Chemist, for instance, dreamed of a snake holding its tail in its mouth, and through the interpretation of this image gained insight into the structure of the benzene ring.

## INSIDE WOODY ALLEN

**34. Inside Woody Allen** by Stu Hample, ©King Features Syndicate, Inc., 1979, used with permission.

# Creative Imaging

We know that creativity is a brain function. But exactly *how* the brain functions during its creative phases is still largely a mystery. It seems, however, that the creative imagination operates by the interplay of several key functions: (1) *synthesis,* the mind's ability to form unified patterns out of the chaotic input and multiplicity of stimuli; (2) *simplification,* its ability to reduce complexitites to essences and basic elements; (3) *detachment,* the disassociation of leftbrain thinking that allows insights to occur from the more intuitive rightbrain; (4) energizing, activating the mind towards making new connections, reassociations, and modifications.

The French Mathematician, Jules Henri Poincaré, likened the mind's search for creative solutions to that of the interaction of atoms: "They plow through space in all directions . . . their mutual collisions may produce new combinations." He also stressed the importance of the *prepared* mind, however, and viewed the conscious mind (with its acquired skills and knowledge) as the prod that liberates the fixed structures of the unconscious so they can move toward new combinations.

Other writers have described the creative operations of the mind as a function of these processes: preparation, incubation, illumination and verification.

For further reading on this subject, consult Alex F. Osborn's authoritative text, *Applied Imagination,* published by Charles Scribner's Sons, New York.

# The Split Brain

Neurophysiologists today claim that the cerebral cortex of the human brain is in reality *two* brains — composed of the left and right hemispheres — each having distinctly different functions. They interact through interconnecting fibers known as the corpus callosum. Although the two hemispheres of the brain seem to have equal potential to perform all mental functions, each has its special operations. The right part of the brain controls the left part of the body and vice versa. The left brain controls rational, analytical thinking, language skills, mathematical functions, and sequentially ordered thinking. The right brain, on the other hand, controls intuitive functions, spatial orientation, spatial constructions, crafts, skills, art, music, creative expression, and the recognition of images. The right brain processes data simultaneously and more diffusely than the left, tending to evolve holistic mental patterns.

Research psychologist Robert Ornstein suggests that because of the brain's special makeup, there are two major modes of consciousness that simultaneously coexist within each person: the rational and the intuitive. Supporting this hypothesis is Anton Ehrenzweig, author of *The Hidden Order of Art,* who states that the coordinated efforts of *unconscious* mental scanning, combined with *conscious* differentiation allows the artist to bring forth to the surface the "hidden order of the unconscious." This coordinated mental activity should be considered a "precision tool" for creative thinking, and should be nurtured by practice and application.

Thus, creative imagination involves more than just having images in the mind's eye; it is a process of *sensing relationships between diverse elements,* which results in the formation of new and unexpected metaphors. As Jean Paul Sartre wrote, "the imagination gives clarity to perception." In itself, imagination is not constructive. Only when the products of imagination and fantasy are linked with conscious perception and deliberation does formative thinking and creative vision emerge.

Intuition, the process of subjectively sensing insights without benefit of rational thought, is a natural and subconscious form of intelligence. However, when rational intelligence is used to "nail down" intuitions into objective perceptions, they cease being intuitions and become absorbed into the patterns of conscious experience.

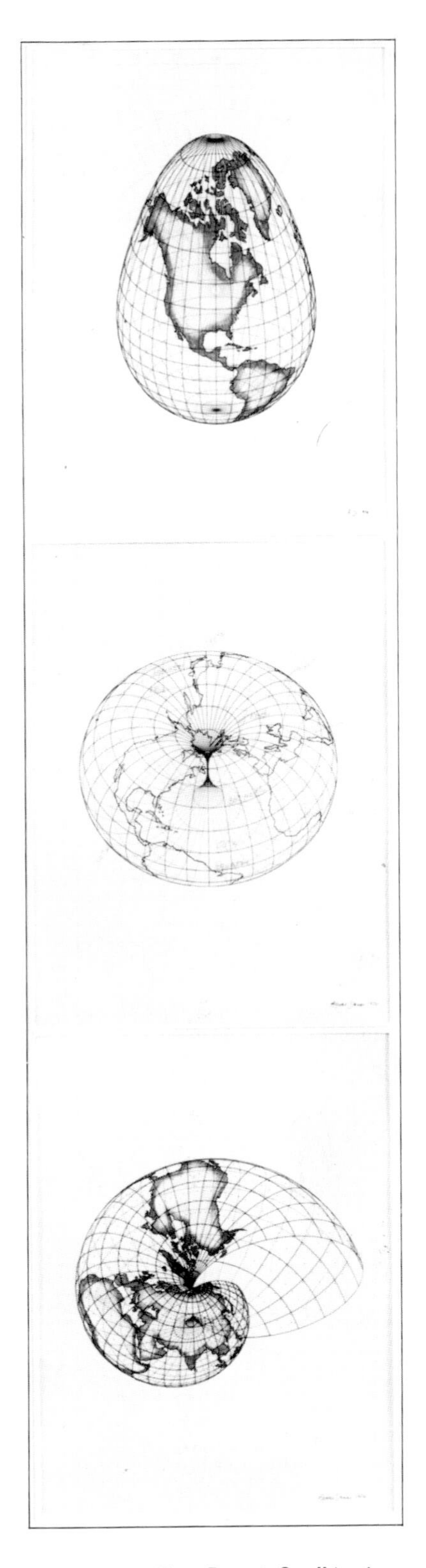

**38. Earth as Egg, Donut, Snail** by Agnes Denes, 1974, ink and charcoal on graph paper. Courtesy the artist.

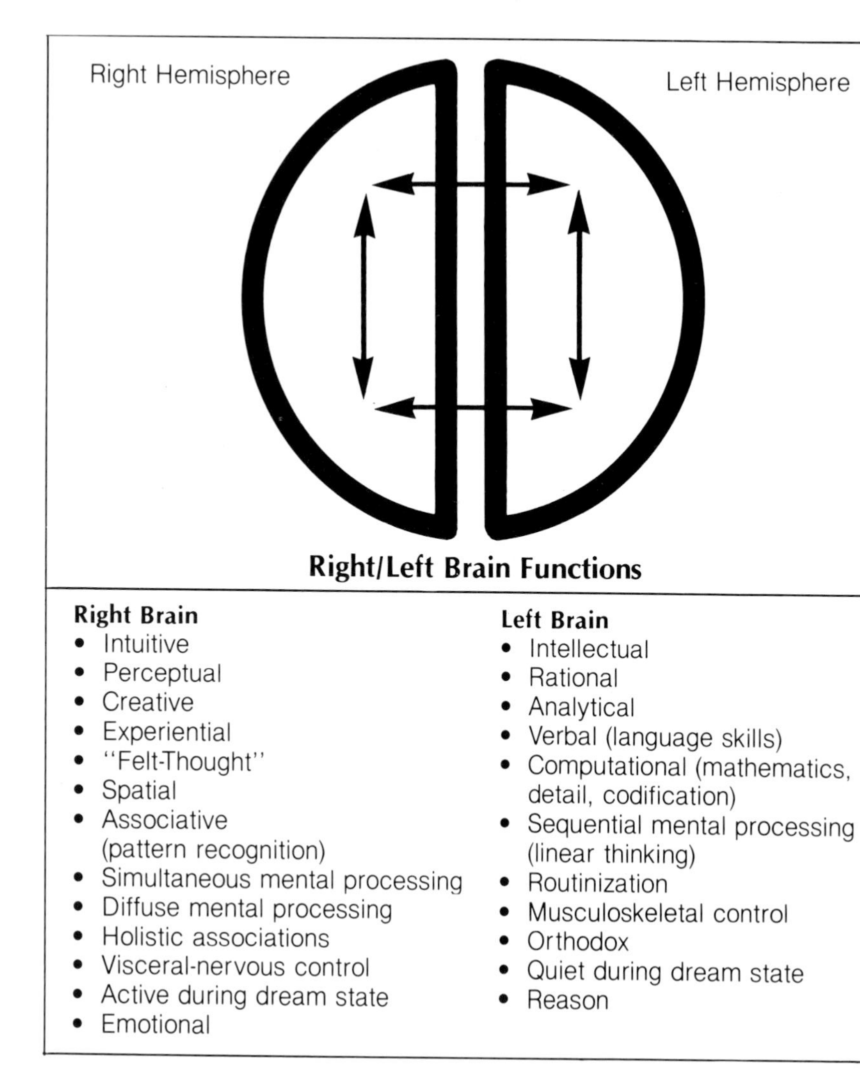

**above: 39. Chair Transformation** by Lucas Samaras, 1970, 38" x 20" x 20" (96.5 x 50.8 x 50.8 cm), white Formica and colored yarn. Courtesy Pace Gallery, New York.

## Mobilizing Creative Thinking

The following attitudes and activities seem to be necessary to creative thinking, and have been observed in all truly creative people regardless of profession.

- The training and practice of activities that largely involve rightbrain functions.
- Suspension of judgment; making disconnected jumps in thinking (lateral thinking).
- Openness to new stimuli, new ideas, new attitudes, new approaches.
- Willingness to take risks; making "leaps of faith"; lessening inhibitions.
- Freedom in subjective thinking; expression of emotions and personal realities.
- Intuitiveness, "playing hunches" to generate spontaneous ideas.
- Freedom to make outlandish responses; rejecting fear of being "wrong" or unconventional.,
- Rejecting destructive criticism, prejudices, indiscriminate praise.
- A childlike attitude of creative play; tinkering with ideas, materials, structures; a "fun" attitude toward experimentation.
- Freedom to fantasize, unconventional imagining.
- Divergent thinking; simultaneous processing of ideas; fluency of ideas.
- Acceptance of nonordinary realities, contradictions; ability to tolerate and manipulate puzzles, ambiguities.

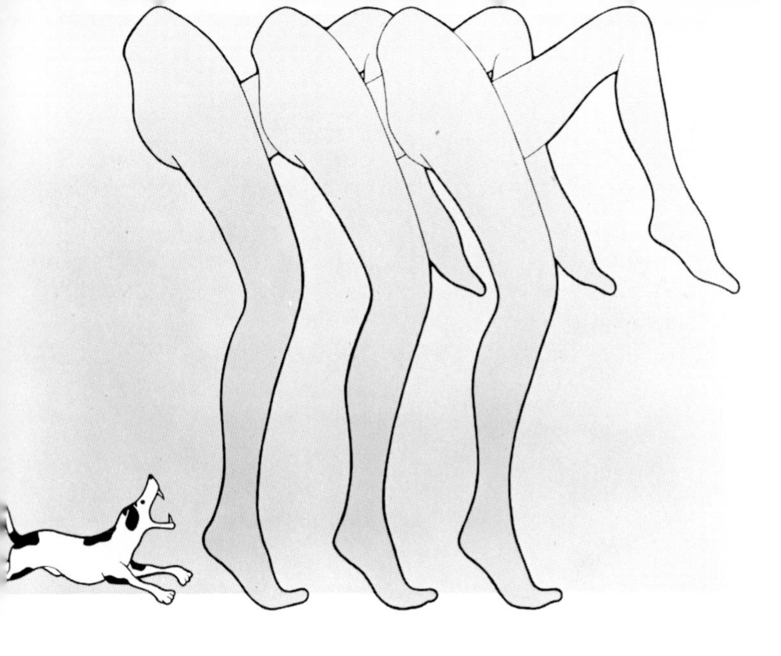

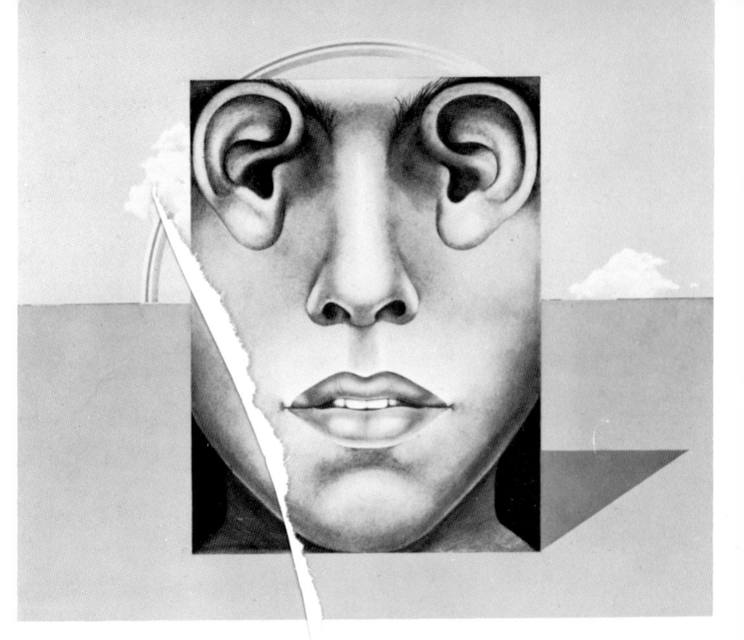

# Transformation: Operational Techniques

How do artists do it? What are some of the underlying methods, techniques, and pictorial devices used to transform ordinary subjects and visual perceptions into uncommon, extraordinary, fantastic ones? Study the works of modern and traditional artists for this purpose. Here are eighteen ways that have been used successfully and continue to be part of the artist's repertoire:

1. *Magnification:* The "reconstruction" of a subject on a much larger scale than that of the original; for example, a pencil sharpener, eight feet high as a subject for sculpture.
2. *Minification:* Making an object appear smaller; for example, an "art museum" created the size of a shoe box.
3. *Multiplication:* Repeating images or forms within a composition, a grid structure, a kaleidoscopic pattern, in reflected images, et cetera.
4. *Substitution: Changing the original qualities of objects and surfaces: a "soft" telephone, a "wooden" lightbulb, a "concrete" pillow, et cetera.*
5. *Reversals:* Reversing color, perspective, functions, relative sizes and so on; reversing the "laws of nature," such as gravity, et cetera.
6. *Fragmentation:* Splitting or fragmenting objects or images. The subject may be either partially developed, fragmented, or dismembered. Splitting planes, as in Cubist art.
7. *Partial Delineation:* Drawing, carving, or presenting only a portion of an image in its finished state; depicting an image emerging or becoming engulfed in its environment — Michaelangelo's unfinished *Slaves,* for example.
8. *Distortion:* Changing an object or image by deformation, distortion, or progressive states of degradation: burned, dissolved, decomposed, crushed, cracked, et cetera.
9. *Disguising:* The use of latent or hidden images; obscuring the qualities of an object by wrapping, masking, or camouflaging.

**above left: 40. Let's Get Out of the Hall** by John Wesley, 1971, 36" x 47" (91.4 x 119.4 cm), acrylic on canvas. Courtesy Robert Elkon Gallery, New York. An isolated set of dancing legs is chased by a barking dog. Through use of fragmentation, Wesley has created a paradoxical situation.

**above right: 41. Eyes As Ears** by Ute Osterwalder, Courtesy the artist. Relocating anatomical features produces both surreal and symbolic associations in this composition.

**42. Blueberry Pie** by Vivien Thierfelder, soft sculpture with mixed media. Courtesy Alberta Culture, Edmonton. Lush satin berries in a glass beaded crust are topped with a dollop of nylon stocking vanilla ice cream.

10. *Metamorphosis:* Depicting images or forms in progressive states of change.
11. *Transmutation:* A radical form of metamorphosis; creating Jekyll-and-Hyde transformations, mutations, alterations, hybridizations, re-materializations.
12. *Simultaneity:* Presenting several views or time modes simultaneously; for example, simultaneous presentations of side, top, back, and bottom views, as in Cubist painting; temporal dislocations, such as the simultaneous presentation of childhood and adult memories or various time-space situations; simultaneous presentation of different sensory experiences.
13. *Soft Focus:* Changing focus of all or parts of an image; blurred edges or contour lines; photographic images blurred by movement or panning.
14. *Transference:* The intrusion of an object or element into a space or environment not normally its own; the displacement of an object or elements into a new situation. For example, a huge egg towering above the skyscrapers of New York City's skyline.
15. *Collapsing Volume:* (or vice-versa: expanding two-dimensional forms into three-dimensional objects): Rendering three-dimensional subjects to appear flat or transparent, through the use of contour line, silhouette, transparent planes, et cetera. And the reverse: a well-known painting interpreted as a three-dimensional form.
16. *Animation:* Inanimate subjects can be made "to come to life": organic or inorganic subjects can be given human qualities. Functions can also be implied through image repetition and progression; for example, overlapping silhouettes of scissors in various open and closed positions to suggest "cutting."
17. *Progressive Image Breakdown:* Subjecting an image to treatment that tends to deteriorate, obscure, or progressively break it down to simple shapes or patterns: using transluscent collage overlays to obscure images; sequential color photocopying to break down detail; gridding and transforming; computer serialization; et cetera.
18. *Positive-Negative Reversal:* Using the photographic negative rather than the print (or *both)* in a composition; using female molds or *concave* shapes to abstract figurative sculpture (as in the work of Alexander Archipenko and Cubist sculptors).

**above left: 43. Zipper II** by Leonard Kocianski, 1979, 41" x 29" (104 x 73.6 cm), pastel on paper. Courtesy George Belcher Gallery, San Francisco.

**44. Metronome** by Andre Peterson, 1975, 30" x 30" x 72" (76.2 x 76.2 x 182.8 cm), Birch, Oak. Courtesy the artist.

# 2

## ACTIVITIES

### 2-1 / Eidetics

**Concept:** Strengthening visual recall.

**Do:** 1. Contemplate the images on the grid (right) for one minute.

2. Close the book. On a piece of paper, draw the grid and the images in their correct positions.

3. Create a visual recall exercise of your own.

### 2-2 / Visualization

**Concept:** Sharpening abilities to form mental images.

**Do:** 1. Look at the image of the black circle on the white background for one minute.

2. Cover the image with white paper. Imagine the black circle in your mind's eye.

3. Imagine the circle splitting in half vertically, producing two half-circles.

4. Imagine the two black half-circles suddenly turning a brilliant orange with white polka dots.

5. Imagine the half-circles turning into the wings of a butterfly.

6. Imagine a butterfly with wings of bright orange and white dots — and a black shiny body.

7. Imagine the butterfly flying away.

Rate yourself: Images were very clear (C), vague (V), indistinct (I).

8. Create an imagination exercise of your own.

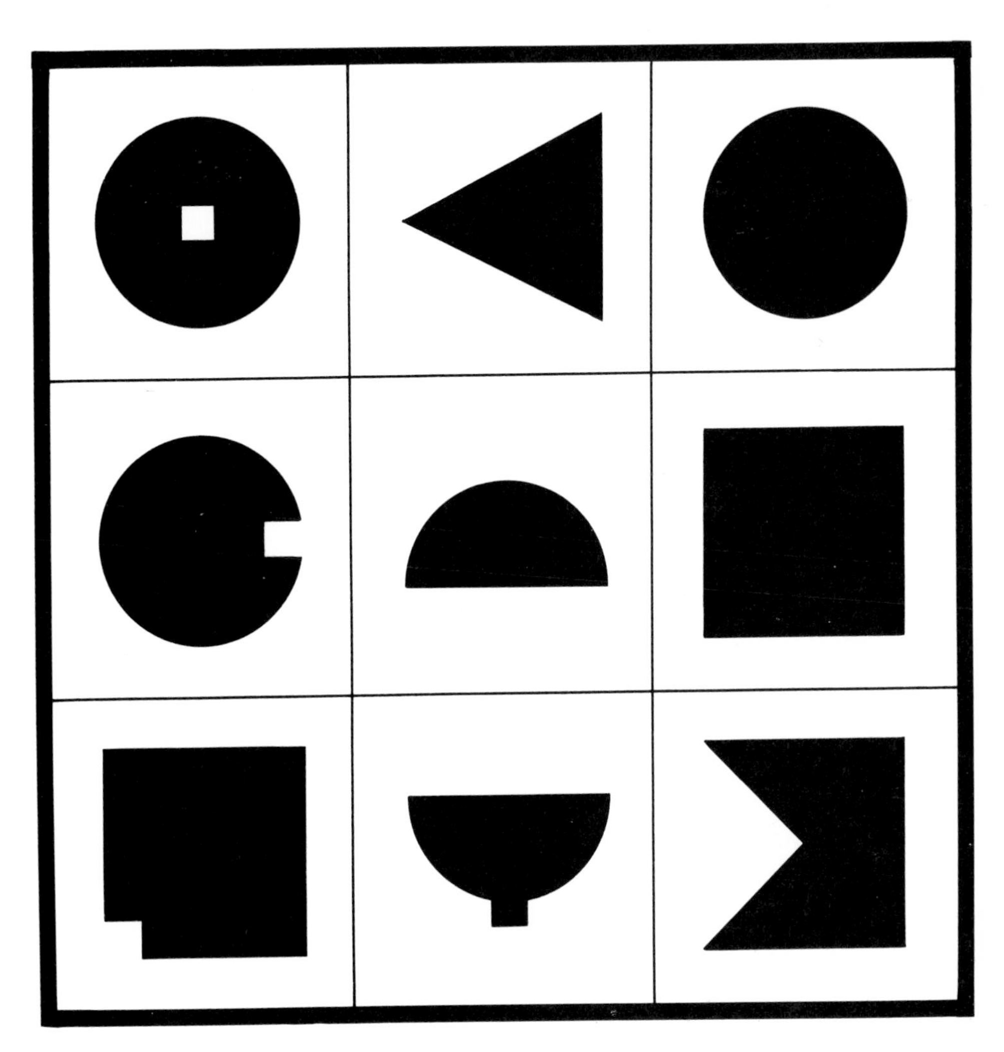

**above: 45, 46.** Eidetic exercises for strengthening visual recall.

## 2-3 / Memory Test

**Concept:** Sharpening eidetic recall.

**Do:** 1. Study an art reproduction carefully for three minutes.

2. Remove the reproduction and write down as many details as you can remember regarding the components of the composition.

3. Check your memory by referring back to the reproduction.

## 2-4 / "Wouldn't it be a strange world if. . ."

**Concept:** Mobilizing fantasy; arresting or reversing "laws of nature."

**Do:** 1. Make up a list of 10 "impossible situations" based on your reactions to "Wouldn't it be a strange world if. . ."

2. Make a drawing, cartoon, collage, or painting that depicts one of your ideas.

**47. Raining Cars** by Randall Rosenthal, acrylic. Courtesy Galerie Jasa, Munich. Wouldn't it be a strange world if suddenly it rained cars? With poetic license the artist does the impossible: commonplace objects are juxtaposed to create strange, surreal environments.

## 2-5 / Selected Segment

**Concept:** Searching for design with a viewfinder.

**Do:** 1. Select a commonplace object as a subject for this composition — scissors, key case, egg beater, pliers, key ring, stapler, et cetera.

2. Cut out a viewfinder from cardboard or heavy paper. (Make the window much smaller than the overall size of the object.)

3. Scan the object for an interesting compositional segment.

4. With the viewfinder in place over the object, draw an enlargement of the selected segment.

## 2-6 / Minification

**Concept:** Changing perceptual responses to a subject through miniaturization.

**Do:** 1. Make a miniature art museum.

2. Collect images from magazines and interesting three-dimensional objects for the "collection" of your museum.

3. Subdivide a small chest of drawers or other appropriate containers to act as the museum.

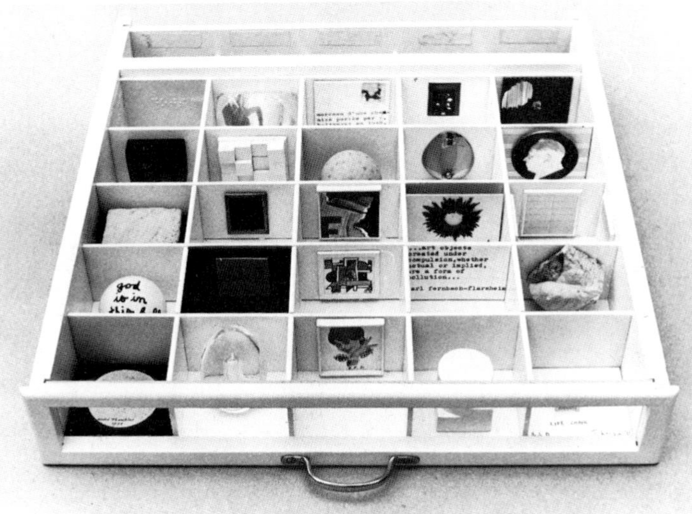

**48, 49. Miniature Museum of Modern Art** by Herbert Distel, 1970. Courtesy the artist. This miniature "art museum" has a collection of *objets d'art* carefully arranged within the cells of each drawer.

## 2-7 / Impossible Realities

**Concept:** Sharpening ability to form mental pictures.

**Do:** 1. Visualize the following structures in your mind's eye:

A chair made of Ping-Pong balls.
An automobile made of postage stamps.
A flower made of pencils.
A human head made of clouds.
A hand made of marbles.
A telephone made of ears.
A truck made of lips.
A table made of flowers.
A human figure made of eyes.

2. Rate yourself according to the clarity of your imagery: (C) clear, (V) vague, (I) indistinct.

3. Make up a list of 10 additional "impossible realities."

4. Project assignment: Choose one theme from the group and realize it in tangible form by creating a collage, drawing, bas-relief design, or sculpture.

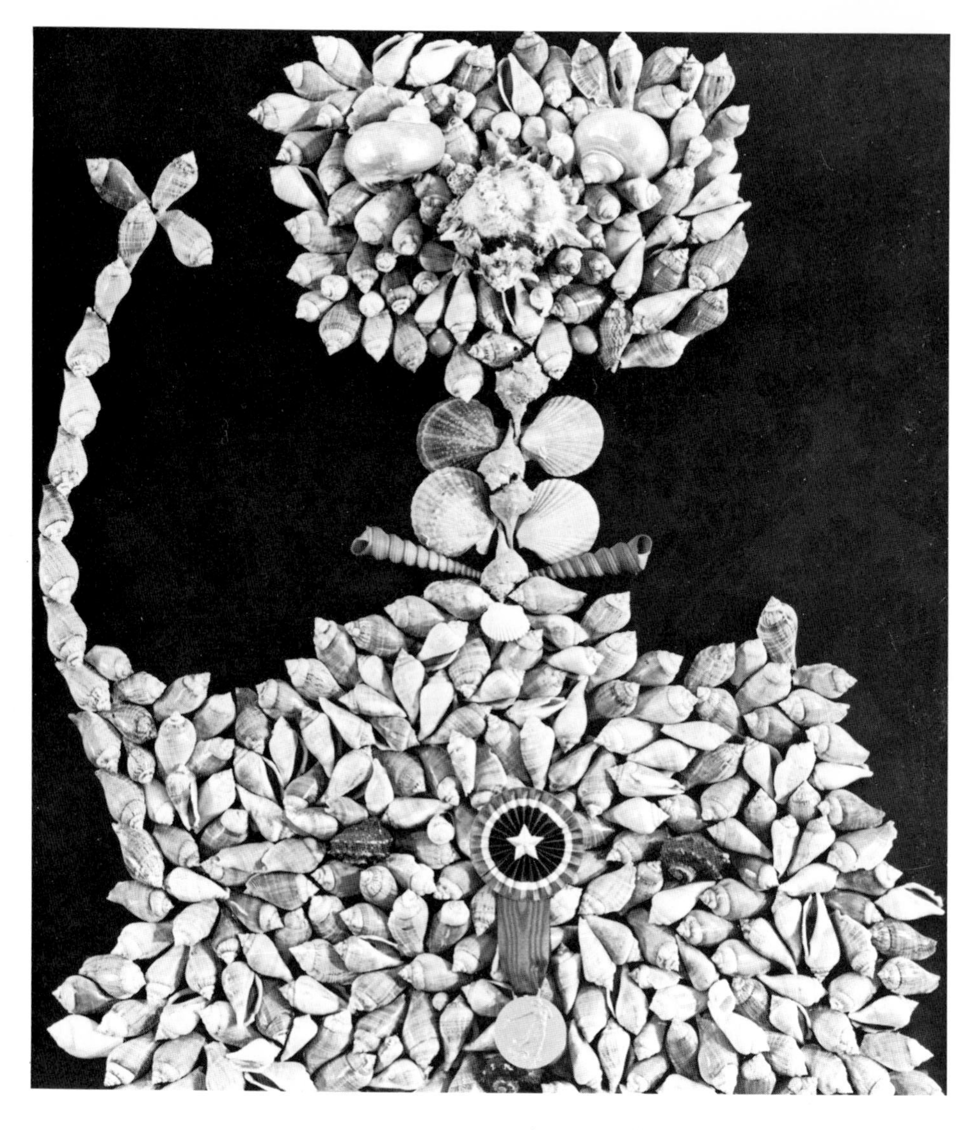

**above: 50. Catherine Henriette De Balzac** by Enrico Baj, 1978, shells, mixed media. Courtesy Arras Gallery, New York.

## 2-8 / Mental Imagery

**Concept:** Sharpening ability to form mental pictures.

**Do:** 1. Contemplate the image to your left. (Turn the page any way you like.)

2. Mentally transform it into another subject.

3. Place tracing paper over the image and carefully trace it. Draw additional lines to transform it into something radically different. (Make three different transformations from the same subject.)

4. Find other images of commonplace objects from books or magazines and create additional transformations.

**left: 51.** An image for visual transformation. What can it become?

## 2-9 / Animated Object

**Concept:** Imbuing inanimate objects with human characteristics.

**Do:** 1. Find an interesting discarded object: an old radio, steam iron, telephone, tea kettle, et cetera.

2. Add features: eyes, nose, mouth, ears, hair, and so on, using wadded paper and masking tape, plasticine, jar lids, eyeglass frames, et cetera.

3. Cover with papier-mâché (or J-cloth): cut paper into small pieces; dip into an equal mixture of white glue and water; build up in three to five layers.

4. Decorate with acrylic or tempera paint.

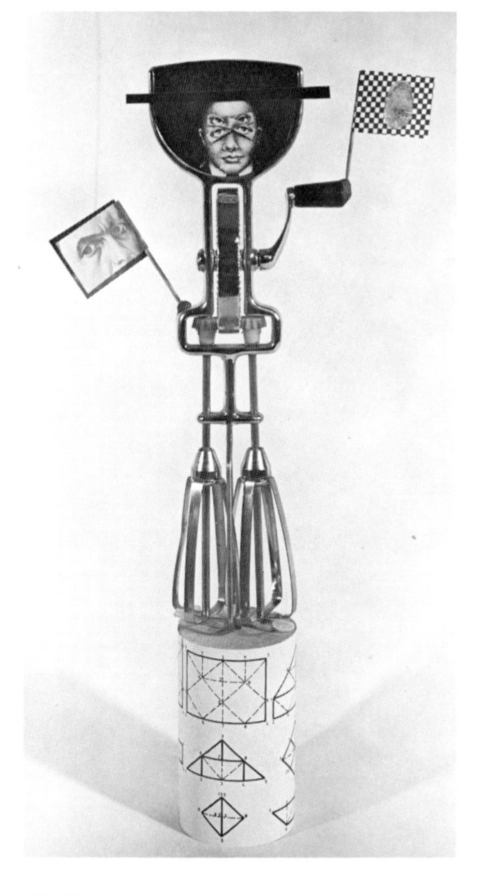

**52, 53. Transformations** by George Geros, mixed media. Courtesy the artist.

## 2-10 / Transforming Derelict Objects

**Concept:** Creating an aesthetic object from an abandoned derelict.

**Do:** 1. Find an interesting object from the garage, attic, flea market, auction, or second-hand store.

2. Transform the object by covering its entire surface with textural materials: mosaic, pebbles, glass, mirrors, feathers, flocking, yarn, paper, sand, photos, rope, coins, marble or granite chips, smaller objects, et cetera. Do this by using white glue: spread glue on the surface, then sprinkle fine-particled materials such as sand, marble dust, or sawdust on it. (Use tile cement to attach heavier materials: butter cement to surfaces, then press pebbles, buttons, or tiles to the surface.)

## 2-11 / Transformation in Nature

**Concept:** Documenting a radical transformation of an environmental object.

**Do:** 1. Select an outdoor subject or a specific marked-off section of landscape for this study; for example: a tree — a building — a small landscape: a 12'' square section of sandy beach — a pebbled landscape.

2. Photograph the same subject three times, making each photo radically different from another due to different environmental conditions brought about by nature or man; for example: light-dark, dry-wet, dry-icy, dry-snow, before-after, radical demolition or alteration, et cetera.

3. Mount the three photographs next to each other on a sheet of mat board.

54. **Staple Remover** by Andre Peterson, 1975, 30" (76 cm) high, Ash. Courtesy the artist. Architectural-size exaggeration of small objects radically affects perceptual responses; small objects are no longer seen in their utilitarian role.

## 2-12 / Magnification

**Concept:** Changing perceptual responses to an object by making it larger.

**Do:** 1. Select a subject for your composition that is normally quite small, such as a paper clip, nail clipper, wristwatch, corkscrew, electrical or mechanical parts, bugs or other small creatures, et cetera.

2. Recreate the subject on a giant scale: Make a soft sculpture by cutting fabrics and flexible materials, which are then sewn, stuffed, stitched, and decorated; or create a large rigid structure by using cardboard and tape.

55. Two mirrors are taped together to act as an aid for discovering symmetrical design patterns.

## 2-13 / Kaleidoscopic Patterns

**Concept:** Creating design through multiplicity.

**Do:** 1. Tape two 12" x 12" mirrors together so they open like a book.

2. Place the mirrors over various designs you have drawn and study the symmetrical variations that are created by manipulating the mirrors.

3. When a desired composition is achieved, trace the portion of the design between the mirrors on acetate with a felt marker.

4. Make additional tracings of the pie-shaped design on acetate to complete the kaleidoscopic pattern. (Note: every other design will have to be reversed to duplicate the mirror reflection.)

5. Enlarge the design with the aid of an overhead projector, and project it onto a large sheet of butcher paper taped to the wall.

6. Render it in acrylics, tempera, or mixed media.

## 2-14 / Three-Dimensional Projections

**Concept:** Projecting images and patterns on three-dimensional objects.

**Do:** 1. Select a number of still life subjects: bottles, kitchen pots, boxes, old shoes, discarded musical instruments, beach balls, et cetera.

2. Paint them white with acrylic gesso.

3. Project 35mm slides of extreme close-ups (butterfly wings, subjects filmed through microscopes, or slides of Op Art) on to the surfaces of these objects.

4. Draw, paint, or photograph the resultant combination.

## 2-15 / Mutant Fruits and Vegetables

**Concept:** Transforming the appearance of fruits and vegetables. Imagine that some strange, unaccountable force (cataclysmic but not catastrophic) has altered the life-giving rays of the sun and the mineral content of the earth.

**Do:** 1. Imagine what might be the biological and/or physical effects of fruits and vegetables that are grown in the garden of this changed environment.

2. Using clay, handbuild four mutant fruits or vegetables that reflect this phenomenon. Bisque fire and paint with acrylic. (David Furman)

## 2-16 / Re-Materialization

**Concept:** Depicting metamorphosis of an object's surface texture.

**Do:** 1. As a subject for this composition, select two objects: (a) a commonplace object, (b) another object with pronounced surface texture.

2. Make a detailed outline drawing of the first object.

3. Instead of rendering it with its original texture, render it with the texture of the second object; for example: an electric light bulb that appears to be made of wood.

## 2-17 / Growth Patterns

**Concept:** Creating designs portraying progressive states of growth and transformation.

**Do:** 1. In the middle of a 9" x 12" piece of drawing paper, draw the outline of a basic shape — circle, triangle, square, et cetera — or the silhouette of a recognizable object.

2. Draw another line around the original drawing, following the general contours but showing some slight evidence of transformation.

3. Continue drawing additional outline shapes around each preceding drawing, developing a progressive growth pattern from the middle of the page outward. The final outside shape should be quite different from the original shape.

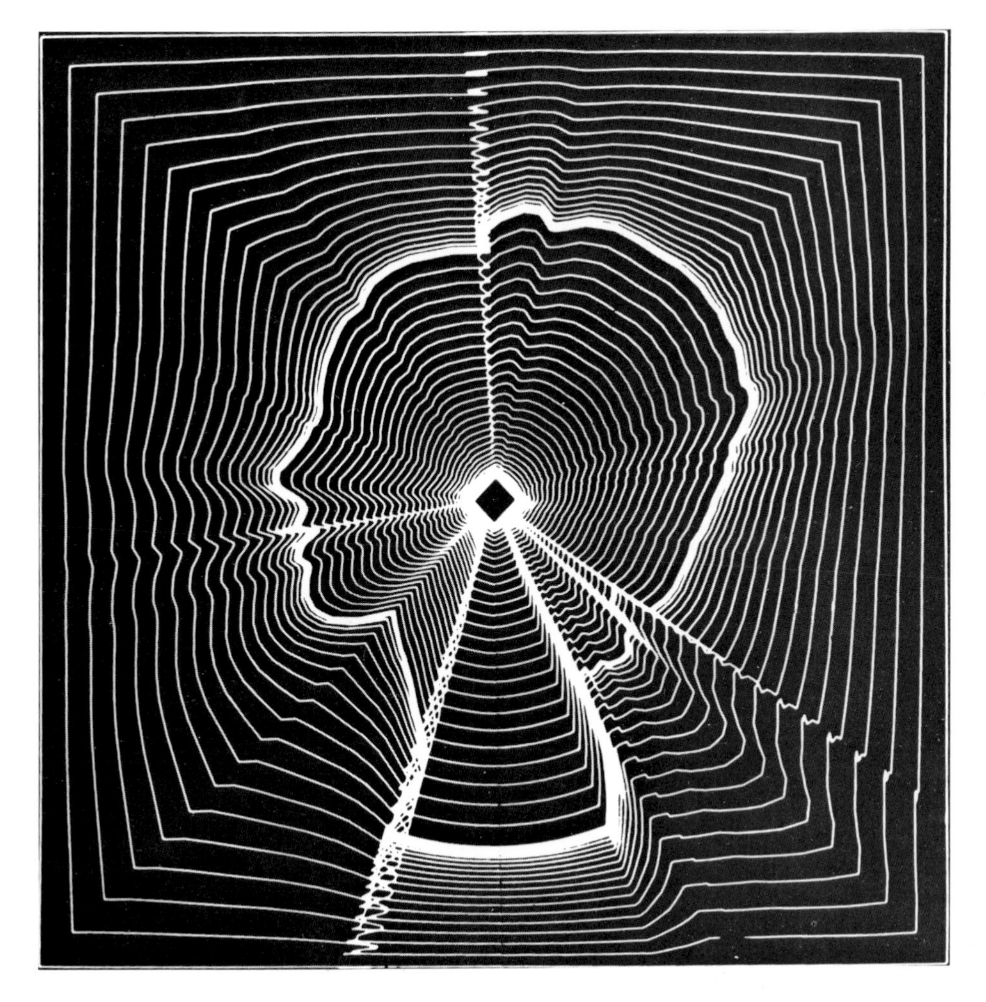

**above: 56. Return to a Square** by Kunio Yamanaka, drawing. This computer drawing presents concentric images of a square that progressively change into a human head, and back again into a square.

## 2-18 / Silhouettes

**Concept:** Compressing volumetric form to flat shapes and silhouettes.

**Do:** 1. Direct a light source (a lamp or spotlight) in front of a subject so that its shadow is projected onto a large sheet of butcher paper taped to the wall. (Use figures in various poses and gestures, and/or inanimate objects.)

2. Trace the outlines of the shadows to the paper. Change positions of the light source to change the quality and size of the projected images; trace these as well.

3. Make a mural. Paint with acrylic or tempera.

4. Variation: Project shadows onto plywood and cut out shapes with a portable saber saw. Cut out additional shapes and nail components together to make freestanding units. Paint with acrylic or tempera.

## 2-19 / New Appendages

**Concept:** Changing perceptions of commonplace objects through the incorporation of a new appendage.

**Do:** 1. Attach a handle, faucet, electric cord, electric switch, et cetera, to an object that normally doesn't have one — can you imagine a faucet on a watermelon, an electric cord on a paintbrush?

**57, 58. Silhouettes** by Mario Cerolli. A floodlight placed in front of subjects is used to cast shadows, which are subsequently traced to large sheets of paper. Combinations of tracings are used to make paintings, reliefs, and three-dimensional constructions.

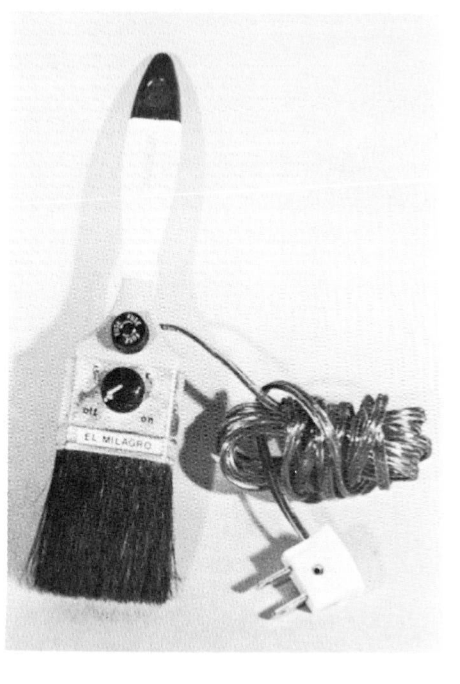


**59. El Milagro (The Electric Paintbrush)** by Bill Meyers, Mixed media. Courtesy the artist.

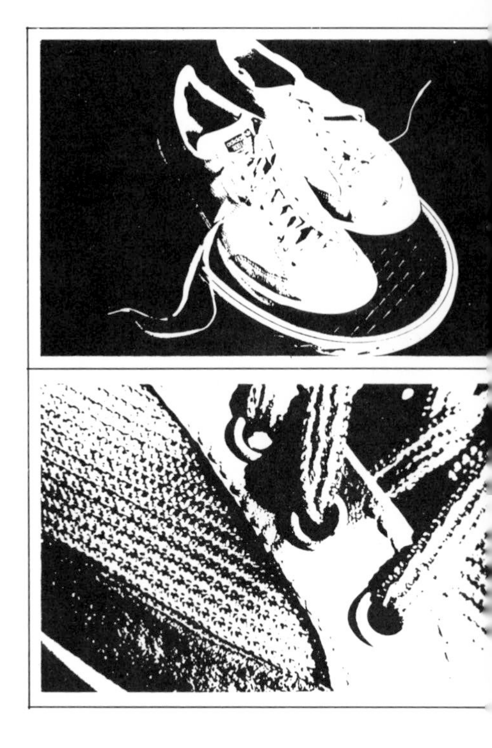

## 2-20 / Zoom

**Concept:** Developing a composition that shows progressive magnification of a subject.

**Do:** 1. Select either an organic or inorganic object to draw.

2. Divide a large piece of drawing paper into nine equal sections.

3. Starting in the top-left box, draw a representational, overall view of the object as accurately as you can.

4. In the next box to the right, imagine that you have a camera with a zoom lens and draw a close-up portion of the object in accurate detail.

5. In the remaining sections, continue zooming in on the object and enlarging finer details. The last frame should be an enlarged detail created with the aid of a magnifying glass or microscope.

**60. Zoom** by Phillip Zane, photograph. Courtesy the artist.

## 2-21 / Design and Function

**Concept:** Depicting the appearance and function of an object within a single composition.

**Do:** 1. Select a commonplace object as the subject for this design project: a pair of scissors, hammer, saw, pencil, bicycle, and so on.

2. Make silhouette or contour drawings of the object in several different positions.

3. Overlap the various drawings and multiple tracings of the object and render in pen and ink.

## 2-22 / Disguising

**Concept:** Altering perceptions of an object through camouflage or disguise.

**Do:** 1. Wrap a three-dimensional object with cloth, thin polyurethane, or some other flexible material.

2. Bind with rope, tape, twine, or wire.

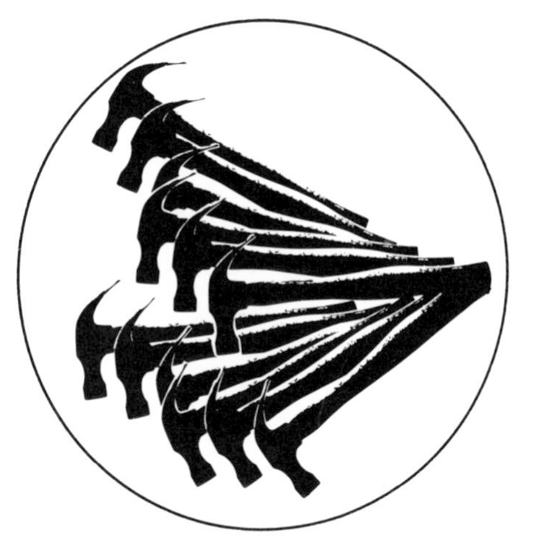

**above: 61.** The form and function of a hammer is graphically integrated in this design.

**above right: 62.** Wrapping and binding commonplace objects automatically transforms them into mysterious forms.

## 2-23 / Metamorphosis

**Concept:** Depicting the transformation of an object from one physical state to another.

**Do:** 1. Select two dissimilar images — one organic, the other inorganic — from books, dictionaries, or other sources for finding graphic images.

2. Starting with the first image, make a series of drawings that depict the image progressively breaking down (in four increments or more) to a geometric shape such as a triangle, circle, diamond or square.

**63. Metamorphosis** by design students, University of Calgary.

## 2-24 / Distortion Grids

**Concept:** Altering images through the use of distortion grids.

**Do:** 1. Cut out a photographic image of a person's head from a magazine, poster, or newspaper.

2. Select one of the three grids shown (right) and subject the image to the distortion it creates.

3. Using a ball-point pen, draw horizontal and vertical lines on the photo 1/4" (6 mm) apart.

4. On a sheet of drawing paper, draw an enlarged version of one of the grids pictured below in light pencil lines, making sure the grid has the same number of horizontal and vertical lines as the photo.

5. Carefully examine each segment of the photo and transfer details to the corresponding segment of the distortion grid in pen and ink.

6. Erase the pencilled grid lines.

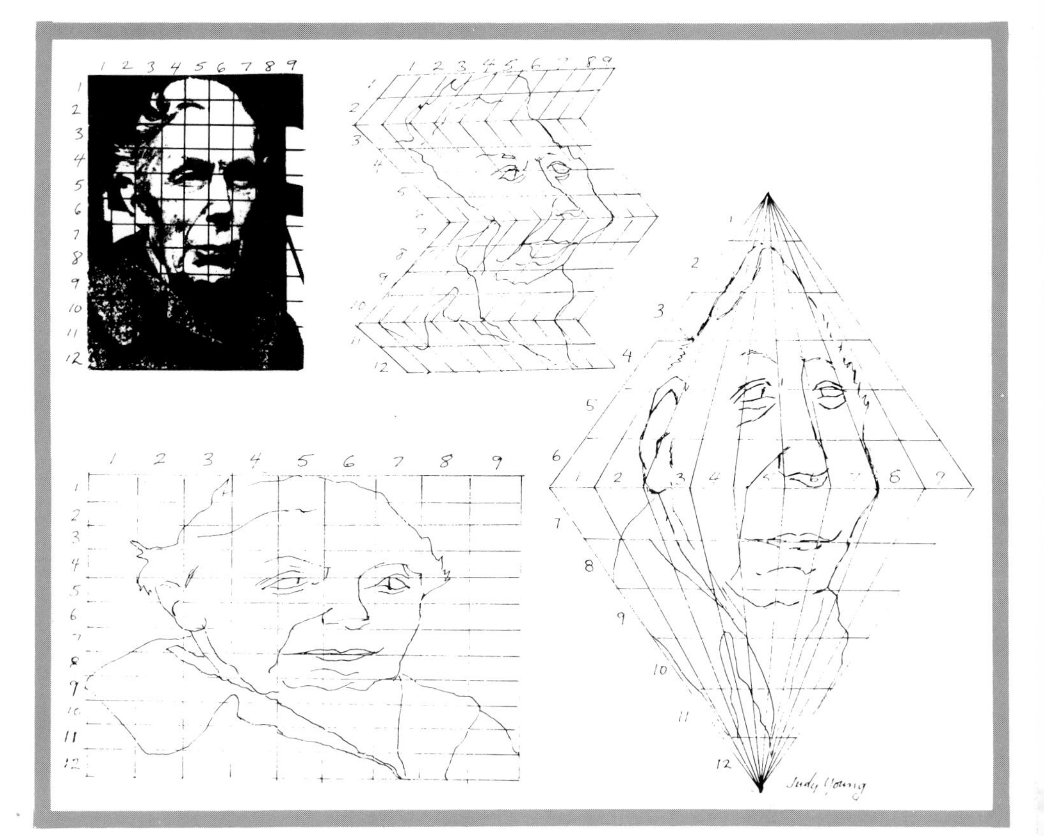

## 2-25 / Hidden Structure

**Concept:** Making structures with concealed elements.

**Do:** 1. Design and make a three-dimensional construction that "opens up" to reveal an interior structure.

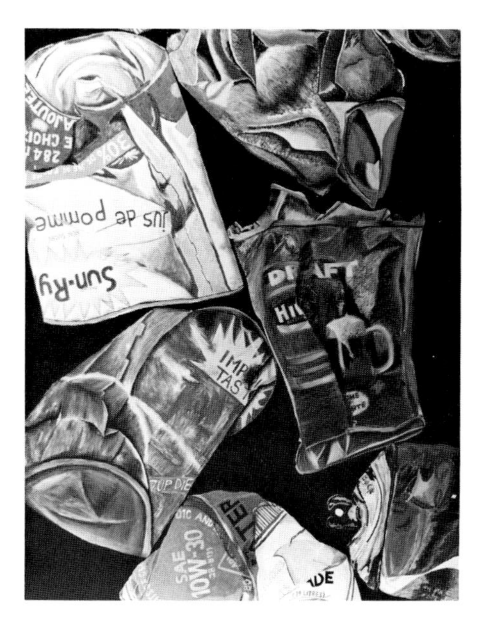

## 2-26 / Art from Scrapped Objects

**Concept:** Making drawings from crushed, rusted, or altered objects.

**Do:** 1. Comb the neighborhood for objects that have been altered by accident, such as soda pop cans crushed by traffic, or altered by effects of nature, such as rusted signs. Look for objects that have been partially burned, broken, crushed, dissolved, or disintegrated.

2. Use the objects as still-life subjects for drawing.

3. Use colored chalk and work big on 30" x 40" (75 x 100 cm) butcher paper. Draw details of the subject but freely exaggerate or abstract the colors.

left: **64. Along the Road** by Tony Urqhart, 1975, 54" (137.2 cm) high, mixed media. Box sculpture that opens. Courtesy Art Gallery of Ontario, Toronto.

center: **65. Crushed Pop Cans (detail of a mural)** by students of Ernest Manning High School, Calgary, Alberta. Courtesy Barry Marks, Tom Hutton.

above: **66. Distortion Grids** by Judy Young, 1980, 8" x 10" (20.3 x 25.4 cm), pen and ink. Courtesy the artist. This work demonstrates three different methods of using distortion grids to enlarge and abstract an image.

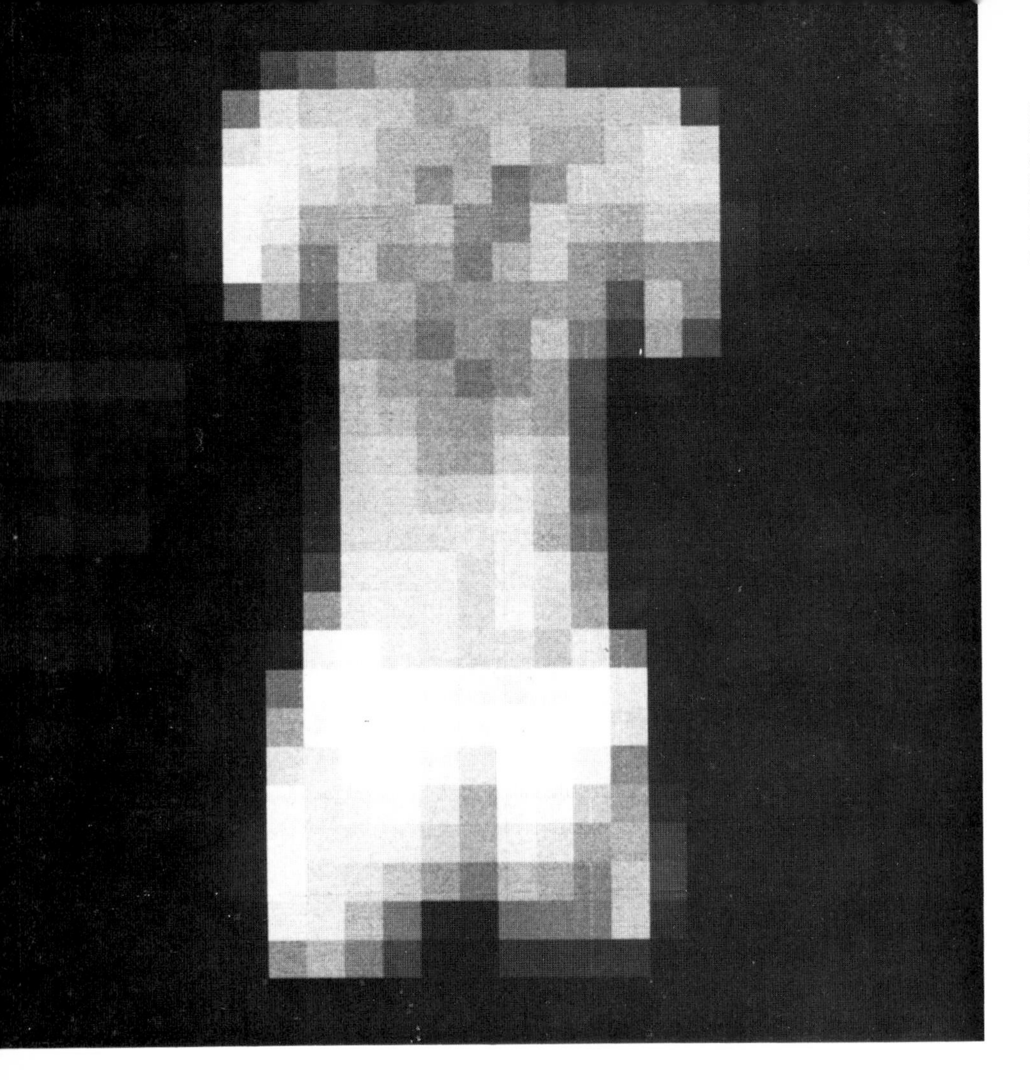

**67. Torso** by Ron Cooper, 1980, lithographic ink on aluminum. Courtesy the artist. A computer-digitized image. Viewed closely, the image is abstract, yet from a distance the fragmented figure pops back into its original representational form. Clarity is also reconstituted by squinting at the image.

## 2-27 / Block Patterns

**Concept:** Breaking down a photographic image into geometric patterns.

**Do:** 1. Select a black-and-white photographic image (a head or figure) from a magazine, newspaper, poster, or an original photo.

2. Tape a sheet of transluscent drafting paper marked in a 1/4'' (6 mm) grid over the image.

3. Study each segment of the photo carefully through the transparent paper. In pencil, render each square with a solid gray tone that represents the average tonality of that square.

4. Continue rendering all the component squares until the composition is complete.

5. Mount on white construction paper or illustration board.

## 2-28 / Select Focus

**Concept:** Making drawings that emulate visual perception.

**Do:** 1. Set up a still-life arrangement.

2. Place a colored tack anywhere on the still life (this represents your focal point).

3. Draw the subject but vary the rendering from very sharp focus (immediately around the focal point) to progressively softer, ''out of focus'' rendering in the peripheral areas.

## 2-29 / Lens Box

**Concept:** Creating kinetic effects with lenticular glass.

**Do:** 1. Create a design, drawing, painting, collage, or photograph. From a local glass shop, obtain a piece of patterned, lenticular, or louvered glass (commonly used as shower glass) cut the same size as your design.

2. Position the glass over the design and slowly move it up and down to determine the most interesting transformation.

3. Measure the distance between the glass and the design. Make a box to hold the design. (The height of the box is determined by the desired transformation).

4. Glue the design to the inside of the box and fasten the glass to the top with fabric tape.

**68. Panoramagram Rotative** by Tim Armstrong, 1968. Courtesy Onnasch Gallery, Berlin. Painted designs are optically (and kinetically) transformed by installing louvered shower glass over the design's surface. Colors and forms optically shift as the spectator moves in front of the work.

**above: 69.** Cast shadows provide a rich source for design experiments.

**center: 70. Design Transformation** by Nicholas Roukes, 1980, pen and ink. Design evolved through analysis and recombination of the shapes found in a telephone.

## 2-30 / Synectic Shadows

**Concept:** Creating designs from cast shadows.

**Do:** 1. Set up a still-life subject such as a houseplant, bicycle, or various kitchen or shop tools.

2. Illuminate the still life with three floodlights that have a red, blue, and green bulb respectively. Notice that the colored lights combine to produce white light. Notice further that the cast shadows are not black, but brilliant hues of magenta, cyan blue, and yellow.

3. Tape white drawing paper on a board and move it behind the still life to find interesting cast shadows.

4. Support the drawing board on a chair and carefully trace the cast shadows with colored chalk. Shift the drawing board and superimpose several drawings to make an interesting composition.

5. Learn more about light color theory and apply the information towards further experimentation.

## 2-31 / Recombining

**Concept:** Analyzing and recombining shapes.

**Do:** 1. Carefully draw the separate parts of an object such as a typewriter, camera, binoculars, egg beater, pencil sharpener, telephone, et cetera.

2. On a separate piece of tracing paper, trace and recombine the elements to produce a unique composition. Combine front, side, and top views.

3. Transfer to illustration board and render with media of your choice.

## 2-32 / Form—Forces—Energies

**Concept:** Creating structures that involve design determined by forces or energies.

**Do:** 1. Create a three-dimensional structure or form based on experiments with one of the following forces:

| | |
|---|---|
| magnetic field | light |
| wind | decomposition |
| gravity | sound |
| organic growth | ice |
| water or fluids | snow |
| chemical action | pressure |

**71. Skypede** by Howard Woody, 1978, mirrorized mylar, nylon, 40" weather balloons, helium. Courtesy the artist. This flying sculpture was inspired by the shape and form of an underwater creature. Constructed of thin segments of plastic that were heat laminated to form a luminous shape, it was inflated with helium. Before launching, a flight pattern was determined and reported to local aviation offices and to the control tower of the local airport. Flights of Woody's inflatables average two hours; this sky sculpture climbed to an altitude of 8200' and traveled 25 miles before finally bursting from atmospheric pressure. The artist says of his work: "My sky sculpture responds to the invisible energies in the atmosphere and gives a visible definition to that energy. The flight life is the sculptural form."

**72. Obelisk** (Magiscope) by Feliciano Bejar, 1967, metal, plastic and crystal lenses. Courtesy the artist. Photo by Bob Schalkwijk.

CHAPTER 3

# SIGNALS, SIGNS, AND SYMBOLS

*The symbol evokes intimations, language can only explain. The symbol touches all the chords of the human heart at once, language is always forced to keep to one thought at a time.*

Jakob Bachofen

Since the beginning of civilization man has relied on signals, signs, and symbols as fundamental tools for interpreting and codifying knowledge and experience. Signals originate in the *physical world* of phenomena, while signs and symbols are *interpretations* of human experience and thus are an important part of human communication.

## Signals

Signals are *biological messages* that are perceived by every organism in nature, including man. These messages are perceived through the senses by means of light, color, temperature, taste, touch, smell, sound, and behavior. In everyday life man receives millions of such messages each day, though most are screened out as undesirable "background noise." Having created his own environment apart from nature, man has grown insensitive to the subtle changes and signals in nature. Wild animals, on the other hand, have maintained their keen awareness to environmental messages in order to survive.

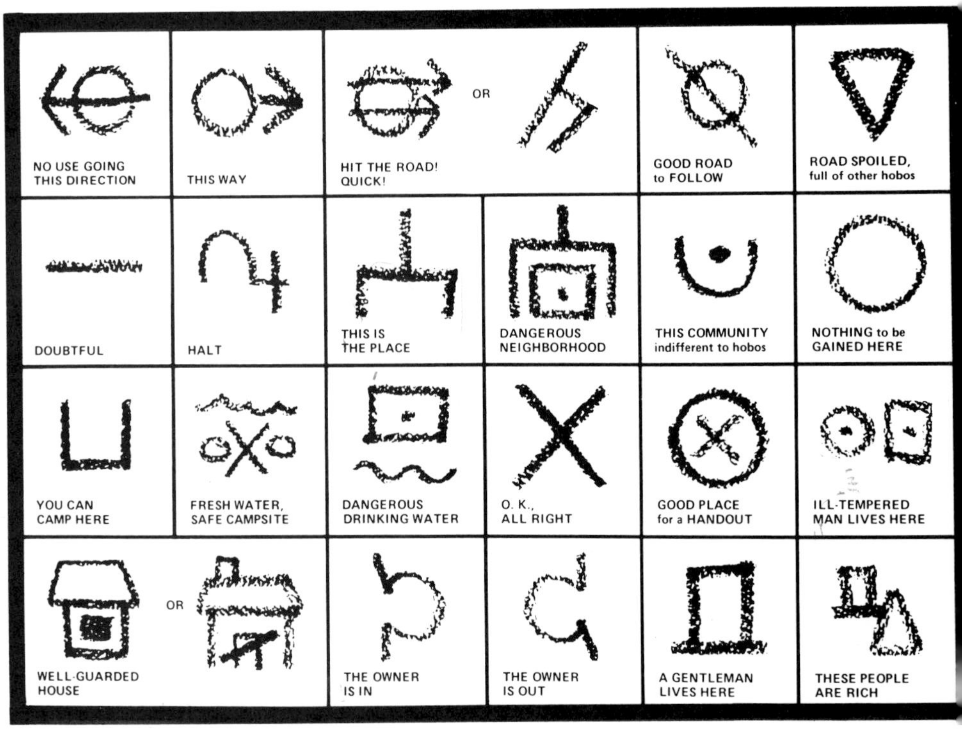

NO USE GOING THIS DIRECTION
THIS WAY
HIT THE ROAD! QUICK!
OR
GOOD ROAD to FOLLOW
ROAD SPOILED, full of other hobos
DOUBTFUL
HALT
THIS IS THE PLACE
DANGEROUS NEIGHBORHOOD
THIS COMMUNITY indifferent to hobos
NOTHING to be GAINED HERE
YOU CAN CAMP HERE
FRESH WATER, SAFE CAMPSITE
DANGEROUS DRINKING WATER
O. K., ALL RIGHT
GOOD PLACE for a HANDOUT
ILL-TEMPERED MAN LIVES HERE
WELL-GUARDED HOUSE
OR
THE OWNER IS IN
THE OWNER IS OUT
A GENTLEMAN LIVES HERE
THESE PEOPLE ARE RICH

**73. Hobo Signs,** from *Symbol Source Book* by Henry Dreyfuss. 1972. Courtesy McGraw Hill, New York.

**opposite page: 74. Giovanni Arnolfini and His Bride** by Jan Van Eyck, 1434, 33" x 22-1/2" (83.8 x 57.2 cm), oil on canvas. Courtesy National Gallery, London. In this double portrait, the artist makes extensive use of graphic symbols: the mirror symbolizes virginity; the sacramental beads indicate dedication to the church and God; the dog, fidelity; oranges, generosity; the bedroom, symbol of the Annunciation; the lighted candle, the presence of Christ; the eggs, fertility; shoes removed, respect for holy ground. Van Eyck's image, along with another "witness," is shown reflected in the mirror. In essence, the painting serves as a pictorial wedding certificate; the signature of the artist is symbolic "witness" to the ceremony.

Johannes de eyck fuit hic

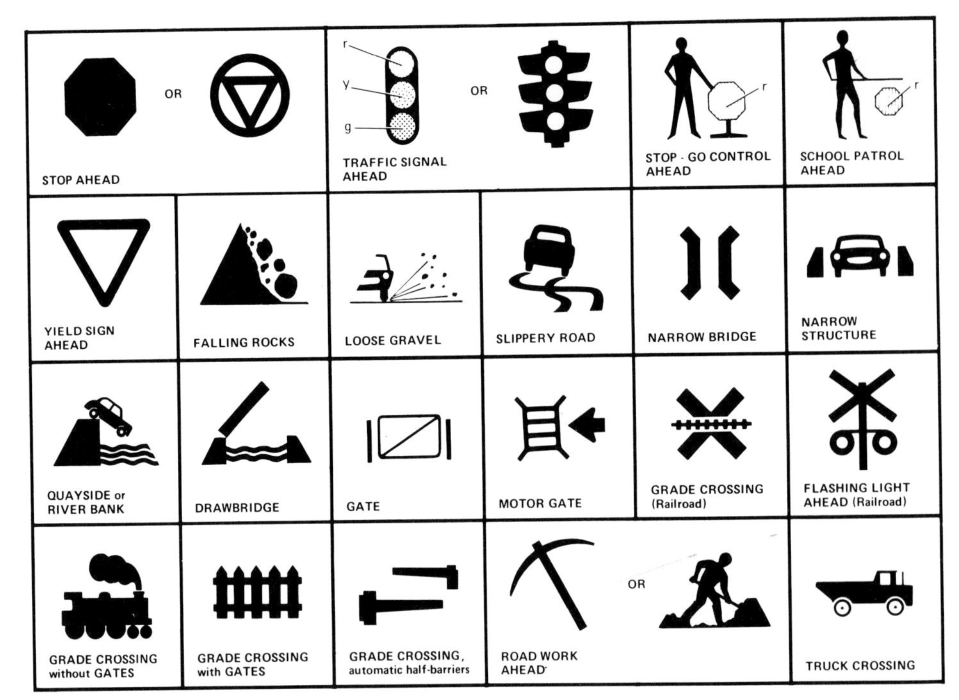


**left: 75. Traffic Signs,** from *Symbol Source Book* by Henry Dreyfuss, 1972. Courtesy McGraw Hill, New York.

**below, center: 76. Trademark** (Wool mark of quality), designed by Francesco Saroglia. Courtesy the International Wool Secretariat.

**bottom left: 77. Mark of Ramses II, King of Egypt, 1324-1258 B.C.** Symbols, Signs and Signets.

# Signs

Signs are signals that the brain interprets as having special meaning. They elicit consistent responses due to our prior experience of the same signals. Signs may therefore take the form of sounds, colors, words, or events. A rustle in the woods, for example, may be interpreted as a sign of impending danger, a black cloud as a sign of a coming storm, smoke as a sign of fire, and so on. There is a distinction, however, between the signs just described and *graphic signs,* which are created and used solely for the purpose of visual communication.

**Graphic Signs.** Graphic signs are visual *simplifications:* they are created to convey complex information in simple, understandable terms. The process by which ideas, information, feelings, and emotions are reduced to simplified graphic equivalents is called *encoding.*

Graphic signs are completely integrated within our social structure; there are particular signs representing every social stratum — from high nobility to lowly peasant — every vocation, every social club, every religion, and so on. A handwritten signature is a graphic sign of personal identity and among other things, serves as a person's guarantee of good faith when attached to a document. Emblems, heraldry, corporate seals, logos, banners, flags, letters, codes, and monograms are other forms of personal or collective identification in symbolic form.

**Codes.** Codes are signal systems with special rules that govern their use. The alphabet, for example (the basis of our language system), falls within this category. In the stricter definition, however, codes are defined as secret information systems — special devices used by trained personnel for purposes of espionage — in which certain signals are memorized and code books kept and referred to for purposes of coding and decoding such secret messages.

**Body Language.** Body language is a silent form of communication, oftentimes unconscious. The quirks and peculiar ways in which we move our bodies — gestures, facial expressions, funny twitches, the way we stand, sit, or walk — are all symbolic forms of communication that reveal a great deal about us to the perceptive observer.

## Symbols

Through intellect and imagination, man transforms his knowledge and experience of the outer, real world and his inner, subjective world into special codes, patterns, and visual configurations that represent reality in abstract terms. A graphic symbol can be defined as a sign or image that expresses meaning *indirectly.*

Symbols are *surrogate images,* insofar as they are "stand-ins" for other factual data. For the artist, symbol-making is a special kind of mental activity whereby complicated ideas and knowledge can be communicated visually through graphic images. Through symbolization, the artist can also communicate desires, fears, anxieties, moods, sensations, feelings, and intuitions. All of these experiences, of course, are subjective or emotional, yet are capable of being graphically equated in line, shape, color, texture, and form. Symbolic communication, then, can take various sensory modes. We communicate verbally with sound patterns, graphically with established visual configurations, tactilely through touch, and so on. The entire spectrum of human learning, reasoning, and communicating is founded upon symbolic operations.

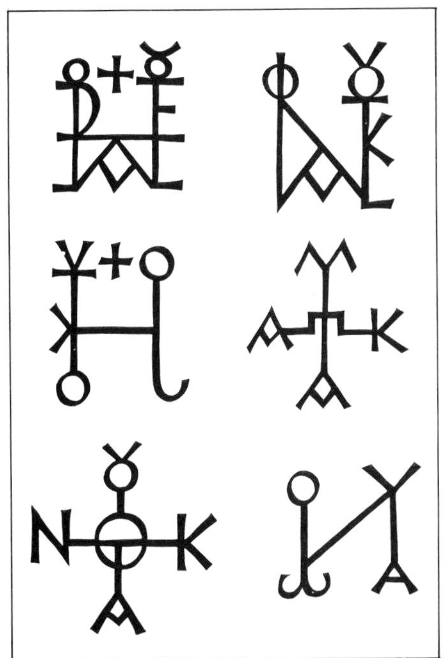

**above: 78. Monograms,** from *The Book of Signs* by Rudolf Koch, 1955. Courtesy Dover, Publications, New York. The Greeks are accredited with inventing the monogram, a graphic device that reached its zenith during the Byzantine period. Early monograms often require interpretation, as they are often disguised, fragmented, or turned back to front.

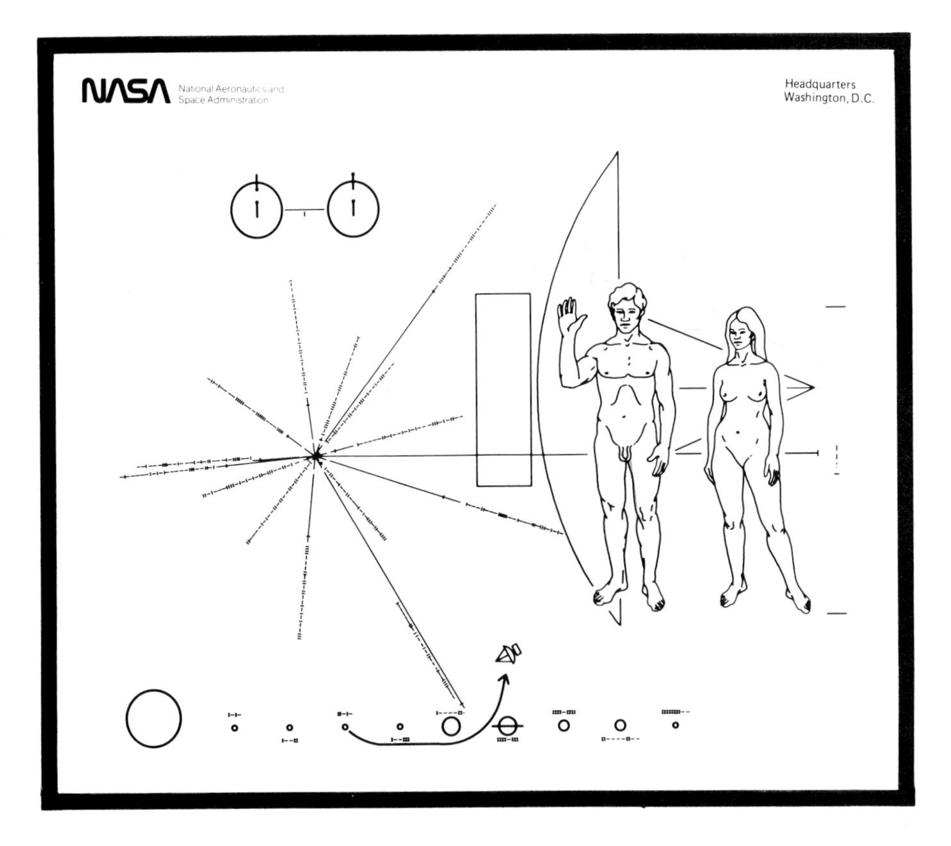


**left: 79. Symbolic drawing.** Courtesy NASA. This drawing, attached to the United States satellite Pioneer 10, was used as an attempt to communicate with "intelligent life" beyond our planet through the use of visual symbols.

**Symbolic Meaning.** Although the meaning of a given visual image may not be deducible to everyone perceiving it, its meaning *is* recognizable to those who have had similar prior experiences or to those who use their imaginations to make coherent mental associations. Consider the disguised symbolism in early Netherlandish painting for example; scholar Rudolf Panofsky interprets the light falling through the window in the *Friedsan Annunciation* as a symbolic metaphor representing the Immaculate Conception.

Likewise, Botticelli's painting, *The Birth of Venus,* portrays a nude figure in a classical pose derived from Greek sculpture. Interpreted symbolically, the nude is considered to represent the Celestial Venus (the nude Venus born of the sea) and simultaneously the Virgin Mary; thus, Botticelli's painting is said to symbolize the concept of *rebirth in God.*

**Symbolic Transformation.** Symbolic transformation happens spontaneously, as the brain tends to interpret any input in terms of symbolic inference. Thus, *every* perception tends to regard the perceived object symbolically. Herbert Silberer, the German psychiatrist, termed this phenomenon as Auto-Symbolization — a mental function that transforms disparities into unified picture symbols. Through symbolic inference, therefore, we are able to mediate experiences from one mental phase to another. It often has been stated, and rightly so, that without symbolism there is no creativity.

**Dream Symbolism.** While asleep, man produces symbols spontaneously, and unconsciously, in the form of dreams. Freud claimed dream symbols are substitutes for original experiences that have been repressed because "they could not be consciously faced." He maintained that dreams do not express *logical* meaning; rather, the symbolic truth of a dream is psychological and requires interpretation for understanding.

**80. The Sleeping Gypsy** by Henri Rousseau, 1897, 51" x 79" (129.5 x 200 cm), oil on canvas. Courtesy The Museum of Modern Art, New York, gift of Mrs. Simon Guggenheim.

**81. Soft Construction with Boiled Beans; Premonition of Civil War** by Salvador Dali, 1936, oil on canvas. Courtesy Philadelphia Museum of Art, Arensberg Collection. The strange symbols of paranoic dream imagery created by the artist can only be understood through emotional conciliation. Although seemingly paradoxical, the images convey powerful psychological implications.

Erich Fromm cited this phrase from the *Talmud* to make his point regarding the importance of understanding one's dreams: "Dreams that are not understood are like letters unopened." According to Fromm, dream symbolism may not appear logical from the viewpoint of space-time continuity, yet it possesses a language with its own grammar and syntax. Although man may forget this language upon waking, and not understand it in his conscious state, it is completely intelligible while sleeping. Fromm claims that in order to find meaning within dreams, we must learn this language anew — in our conscious state.

Tom Chetwynd, in his *Dictionary for Dreamers,* presents an impressive array of archetypal symbolic images: the dream image of a *room* is symbolic of *mother,* since both are capable of containing the human form; *windows* are described as symbolic images representing the *eyes of the soul; stairs* symbolize *sex; birds* connote *aspiration; gates* portray *paths to the unconscious* (or to the dreamer's desires); and so forth. Similarly, the power of the symbols portrayed in the paintings and sculptures of the Inuits and other native people draws its great energy mainly from the portrayal of dream imagery.

André Breton considered the dream as a touchstone to surreality; in the dream, aspects of the real world are mysteriously recalled yet radically altered by the subconscious.

**Hex Signs.** Colorfully painted on the sides of barns, hex signs can still be seen on the sides of buildings among the Pennsylvania Dutch farms. Although now appreciated solely for their decorative value, these designs were once superstitiously regarded as having supernatural powers capable of attracting rain, warding off lightning, making land fertile, or insuring sunshine.

**Signets.** Signets are private symbols used to "sign" one's name in symbolic form. The signet ring was once a widespread means of authenticating information and guaranteeing privacy. (The ring was pressed into a glob of hot wax, used to seal envelopes and important documents.)

**Fetishes.** A fetish is not a symbol, but an object regarded with awe or fascination for its supposed magical power. With the evolution of religion and formal education, man grew away from his inclination to worship idolatrous objects. As a result, African masks and sculpture, once conceived as fetishes, are now collected as aesthetic objects.

Carl Andre, however, brings a new definition to the word fetish: He describes *all* works of art as fetishes. A work of art, he claims, is a dead, insensate thing that is only endowed with spirit by the artist and the viewer. Andre defines the strongest "art fetishes" as those that touch our psyches most deeply and persistently.

**82. St. Sebastian, No. 2** by Eduardo Paolozzi, 1957, 84-3/4" (215.3 cm) high, bronze. Courtesy The Solomon R. Guggenheim Museum, New York. Photo: Robert E. Mates. Man is symbolized as the ultimate victim of technology — a pathetic amalgamation of mechanical appendages.

**83. God Game** by Wolfgang Behl, 1973, 8' (2.4 m) high, wood. Courtesy the artist. Who does this magus represent? In what way does he play his diabolical "Godgame"?

**Beyond Symbolism.** It must be remembered that artists often create works of art without the deliberate intention of "injecting" specific meaning into each work through heavy-handed use of symbolism or stereotyped analogical references. To paraphrase Douglas Davies (see his *Art Culture,* 1979), the risk of dealing with *meaning* in art is that the work may immediately absorb itself into the world, thus losing its privileged aesthetic shelter. For this reason, artists such as Magritte deliberately employ "the cloak of obscurity" and present ambivalent images that seem to defy logical symbolic resolution, but hit hard on a subconscious level. The viewer is presented the task of subjectively completing the work through intuitive responses.

It has been said that a distinguishing characteristic of many contemporary art forms is that the *content* is presented in the form of *unprocessed data* rather than resolutions. Whether this "data" is perceived as chaotic or symbolically cohesive depends entirely on the personal interpretation of each viewer.

**above: 84. Prodigal's Return** by Carroll Barnes, 1972, 63" (160 cm) high, interlocking wood forms. Courtesy the artist. Abstract forms take on human qualities in symbolizing the concept of reunion.

**left: 85. Beautyway: The Woman on the Train** by Hugh Townley, various woods. Courtesy the artist. The memory of a chance meeting serves as the stimulus for creating this bas-relief wood sculpture.

**above: 86. The Subway** by George Tooker, 1950, 18" x 36" (45.7 x 91.4 cm). Courtesy Whitney Museum of American Art, New York, Juliana Force purchase. Unhappy figures languish in a hostile environment: the artist has generated a potent symbol of man's hostile urban jungle. Feelings of alienation, dispair, suspicion, and fear are all present in this graphic representation.

**87. Fire, Air, Water, Earth Ladders** by Joe Tilson, 1974, 88" (223.5 cm) high, red cedar. Courtesy the artist.

**left: 88. The CPA** by Sidney Simon, 1966, 72" (183 cm) high, black walnut, birch. Collection Israel Katz, New York. Photo courtesy the artist. The "numbers" are shown overcoming the image of man — a strong symbolic portrayal of the erosion of identity.

**below: 89. Lizzie's Dream** (Fall River Legend), by Morris Broderson, 1966, 32" x 22" 81.2 x 55.8 cm), mixed media, collection Agnes DeMille. Courtesy the artist. Hands spell *Fall River Legend* in sign language.

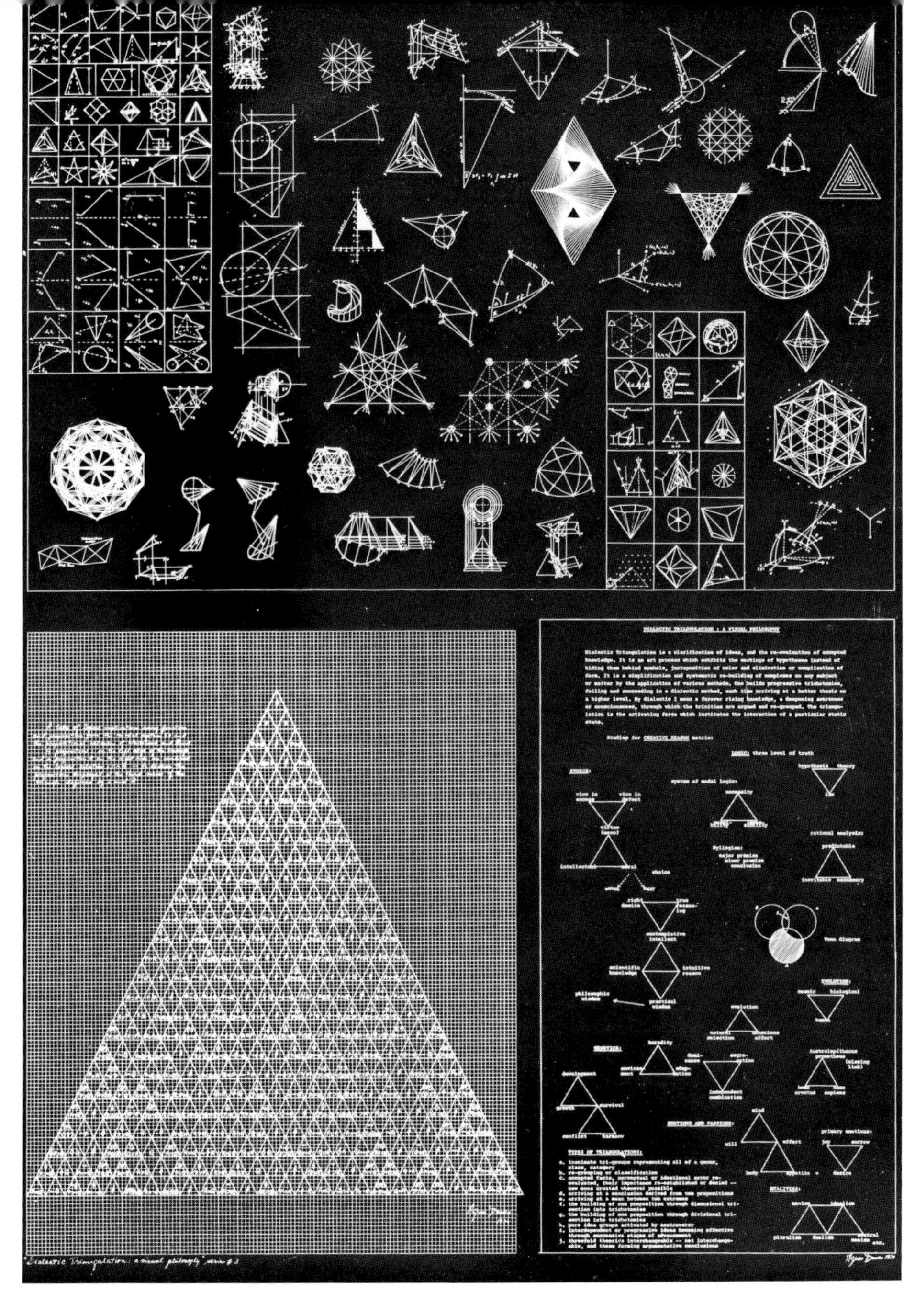

**90. Dialectic Triangulation: A Visual Philosophy** by Agnes Denes, 1969. Denes's work has been described as a textual criticism of the universe, often combining images, X-rays, documentary photography, graphic condensations, signs, maps, and projections. She charts, lists, classifies, and arranges her graphic symbols in an ordered syntax.

**91. Icons to Edward Weston,** from the series *Art in Context: Homage to Walter Benjamin,* ©Manual (Edward Hill and Suzanne Bloom), mixed media. Courtesy the artists.

# 3

## ACTIVITIES

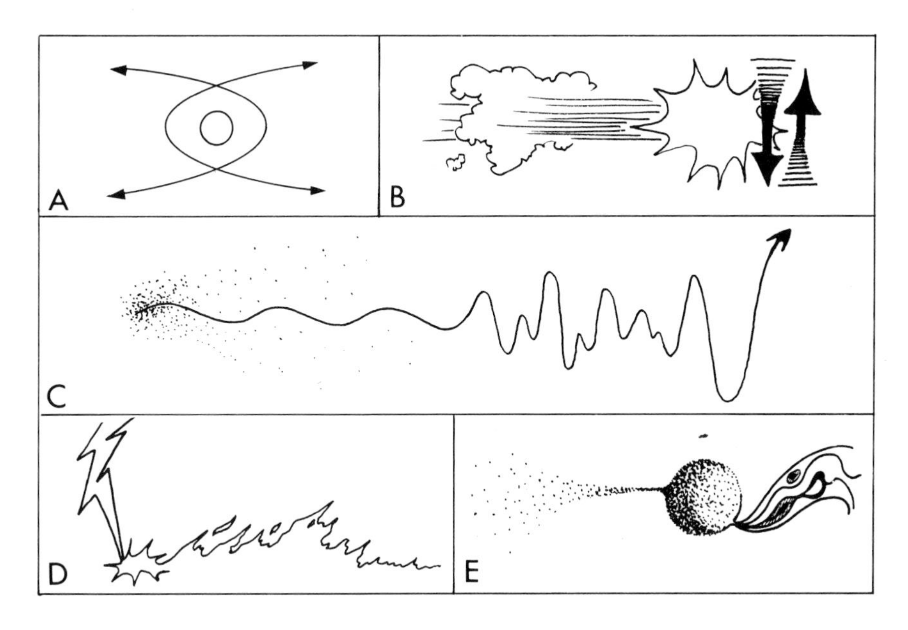


92. **Symbolic Doodles** by Rick Williams, pen and ink. Courtesy the artist. (A) Yesterday - Today - Tomorrow, (B) Compression - Ignition - Exhaust, (C) Sleep - Arousal - Action, (D) Stimulus - Response -Result, (E) Nonbeing - Birth - Transformation.

### What Do These Graphic Symbols Mean?

Match symbol and process: (A) Listen (B) Eject (C) Feed (D) Record

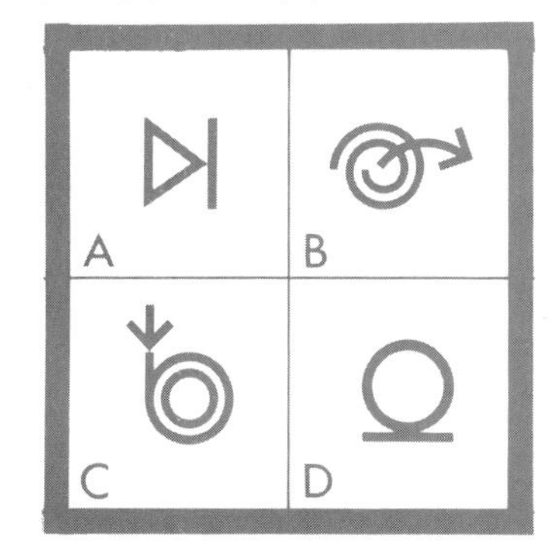


### 3-1 / Symbolization

**Concept:** Creating various graphic equivalents for human and/or mechanical processes.

**Do:** 1. Make a list of "processes"; for example: open, shut, lift, drop, turn, recycle, destruct, do not enter, et cetera.

2. Design an appropriate graphic symbol for each.

### 3-2 / Symbolic Doodles

**Concept:** Exercises in creating graphic symbols.

**Do:** 1. Using a pencil, divide a sheet of paper into six equal compartments.

2. Within each compartment, create a symbolic doodle that portrays each of the following themes:

Yesterday-Today-Tommorrow.
Restraint-Reaction-Freedom.
Sleep-Arousal-Action.
Compression-Ignition-Exhaust.
Nonbeing-Birth-Transformation.
Stimulus-Response-Result.

3. Make up additional themes for graphic interpretation.

**93. Progress of Mankind,** mural by students at Hayward High School, Hayward, California, 4' x 20' (1.2 x 6 m), acrylic on wood relief. Courtesy Hayward Unified Schools.

## 3-3 / Logo

**Concept:** Creating symbols that portray graphic identity.

**Do:** Create your own personal logo, corporate seal, banner, heraldic emblem, or flag. Integrate your initials with abstract shapes, images, design and color to portray aspects of your personality, interests, occupation, hobbies, aspirations, life-style, and so on.

1. Make preliminary sketches with colored pencils on paper.

2. Make a wall hanging of cloth, vinyl, and other fabrics.

## 3-4 / Symbolic Mural

**Concept:** Using symbols as a basis for making a mural.

**Do:** 1. Using the theme Progress of Mankind, research and gather sketches of graphic signs and symbols from various fields of human endeavor: medicine, science, mathematics, sports, art, philosophy, sociology, religion, and so on.

2. Simplify and enlarge the symbols on drawing paper.

3. Trace the symbols onto surfaces of plywood, Masonite, or soft woods.

4. Cut out the shapes with an electric jigsaw.

5. Paint with acrylic.

6. Arrange and glue the shapes to a larger plywood panel that serves as a background. (The mural above was divided into 10 plywood panels, each 24" x 48-1/2" (61 x 123 cm).

## 3-5 / Message

**Concept:** Creating symbols that portray our life-style.

**Do:** 1. Create a symbolic message using graphic designs and images to be carried aboard a spaceship and directed to other forms of intelligent life in the universe.

2. Use the symbols to tell such things as who we are, what we look like, what we do, the things we have created, the places we live in, the technology, science, games, inventions, sports, transportation systems, dances, and so on that are part of our world.

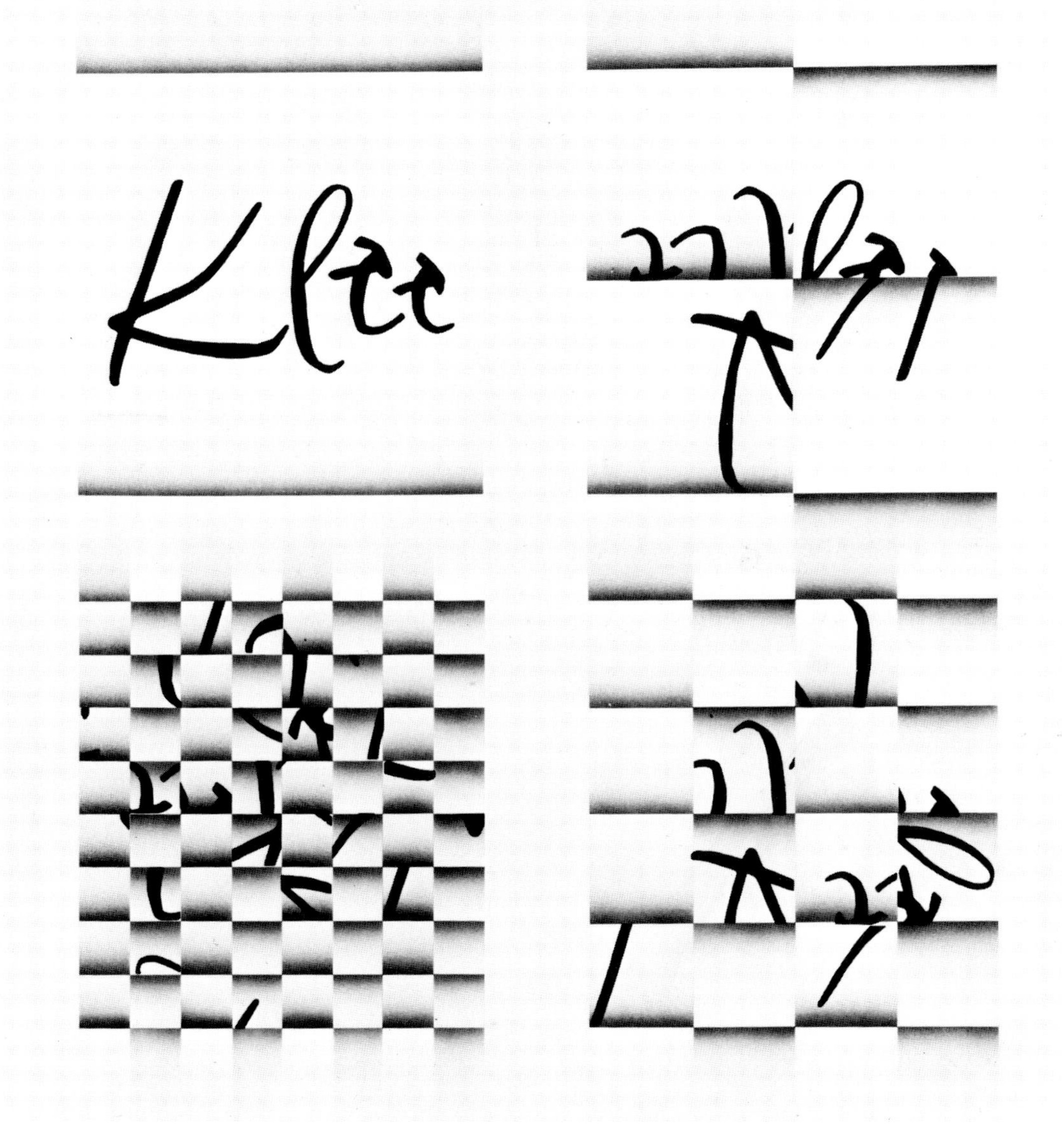


**94. Variations of Paul Klee's Signature** by Bruno Di Bello, 1974, 47-1/4" x 47-1/4" (120 x 120 cm). Courtesy Studio Marconi, Milan.

## 3-6 / Signature

**Concept:** Using calligraphy as a source for making an abstract composition.

**Do:** 1. Sign your name boldly on a large piece of paper with a marking pen. Thicken the letters to create an interesting signature.

2. Grid the drawing into 1" (2.5 cm) squares; mark with ruler and pencil.

3. Cut out the squares and rearrange them on another gridded paper. Arrange the squares in random fashion or use a form of progressive serialization.

## 3-7 / Form and Graffiti

**Concept:** Altering perception of a common object by adding graffiti.

**Do:** 1. Find an interesting object as a subject: an old toy, bottle, rolling pin, toaster, teapot, frying pan, auto part, mechanical device, et cetera.

2. Prime the entire surface of the object with acrylic gesso or white latex paint.

3. Print, scratch, or handletter graffiti over the entire surface of the object. Use letters, numerals, initials, monograms, verse, poetry, calligraphy, or any form of graffiti to embellish the surface.

## 3-8 / Subjective Symbolism

**Concept:** Strengthening intuitive creativity.

**Do:** 1. Arbitrarily cut out one to four lines of text from a magazine article (a provocative statement or portion of dialogue).

2. Make a collage: seek out black-and-white photographs and designs from magazines that you intuitively feel support the text.

3. Use a gluestick and attach the images to a sheet of white drawing paper.

4. Add lines, shapes, tone, and color with pencil, ink, and/or felt-tip pens to heighten the emotional effect and to unify the composition.

Note: Transparent decals can be made from magazine images and superimposed over each other to achieve multiple images. They are made by ironing laminating film over the face of the photographic reproduction and then washing away the backing paper with lukewarm water, leaving only a transparent film with the image on it. Use a gluestick to attach the decals to paper or plastic surfaces. Laminating film is available from graphic art supply stores.

**95. Frost Racquet** by George Geraldi, 1980, mixed media. Courtesy the artist.

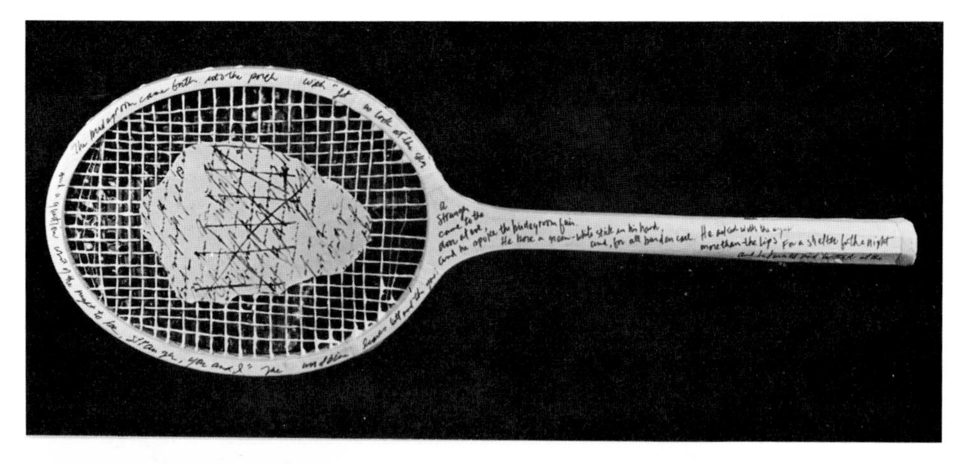

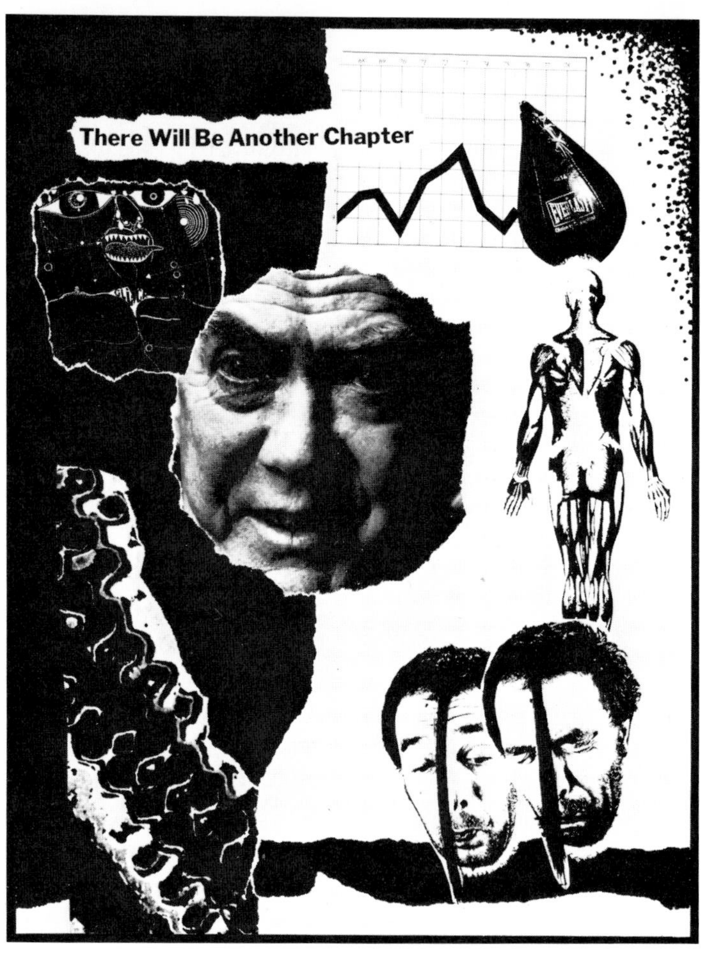


**96. Subjective Collage** by Nancy Groves, mixed media. Courtesy the artist.

## 3-9 / Argument for Social Change

**Concept:** Presenting visual data calculated to alter viewers' attitudes.

Within the realm of conceptual art, artists such as Alan Sonfist often present *informational structures* based on sociological or biological concerns, or based on the creation of new art-language systems. Supported by charts, documents, text, two- and three-dimensional images, this art form interplays disparities between events and conceptions in society, with the ultimate aim of changing viewers' perceptions toward a given subject.

**Do:** 1. Create a presentation that is calculated to focus attention or alter viewers' attitudes regarding a relevant theme, such as: chemical pollution, energy conservation, road safety, male-female dichotomies, justice, ecology, politics, nuclear accidents, nuclear war threat, counterproductive technology, social problems, conservation of threatened animal species, old-age problems, crime, justice and so on.

2. Collect materials and images to present your idea; mix and match photos, maps, charts, documents, notes, two- and three-dimensional materials.

**below: 97. Listen to the Sonar Trees** by David Medalla, 1969, collage. Courtesy the artist. Through a collage of words and images, the artist voices a strong ecological protest.

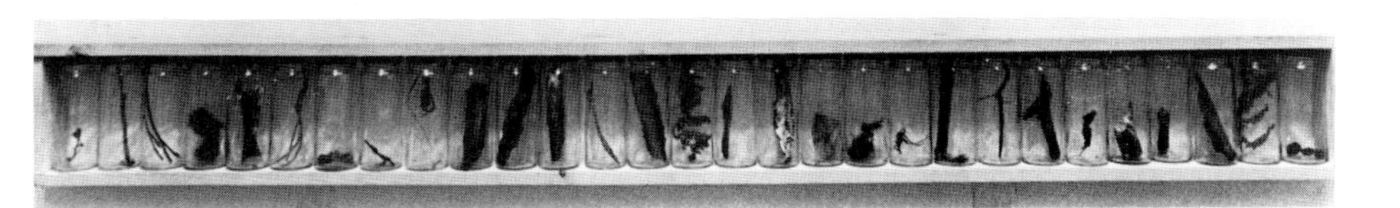

**98. Autobiography of a Forest** by Alan Sonfist, 1969. Courtesy the artist. In his childhood, the artist witnessed the vandalization of a New York virgin forest. Such memories prompted him to create this work — a "pre-colonial" forest. Through such concepts involving the admixture of forms from nature, photographs, and text, he presents a personal message to society: cherish the forest as a natural monument, and re-create the nature we have destroyed. **Autobiography of Hemlock Forest** is a series of unique visual poems — each a collage containing two color photographs of trees, residual material (twigs, earth) from the areas in which the photographs were made, along with a written autobiography of the thoughts, recollections and events which led up to the work of art. Their simultaneous presentation seeks to define the essence of what is, what once was, and what can be a New York City forest.

99. **Gulliver** by Sharon Bombieri, 1980, mixed media. Courtesy the artist.

## 3-10 / Symbolic Shoe

**Concept:** Transforming an ordinary shoe into a symbolic monument.

**Do:** 1. Get an old shoe or boot from the basement, attic, or local flea market.

2. Select a theme from the list below, or make up your own subject.

Ode to Carl Jung
Ode to Lemuel Gulliver
Ode to Napoleon Bonaparte
Ode to Icarus
Ode to Albert Einstein
Ode to John Dillinger
Ode to Mohammed Ali
Ode to René Magritte
Ode to Pablo Picasso
Ode to Roy Lichtenstein
Ode to Salvador Dali
Ode to Marilyn Monroe
Ode to Harry Houdini
Ode to Toulouse Lautrec

3. Embellish the shoe with elements to portray the theme; for example: add papier-mâché wings, roller skates, miniature toys, ladders, lights, taxidermy eyes, sails, transistors, plumbing fixtures, coins, papier-mâché appendages, et cetera. Decorate the surface with bits of mosaic, glitter, yarn, mirror, paint, et cetera.

4. Mount on a base and affix a nameplate to it.

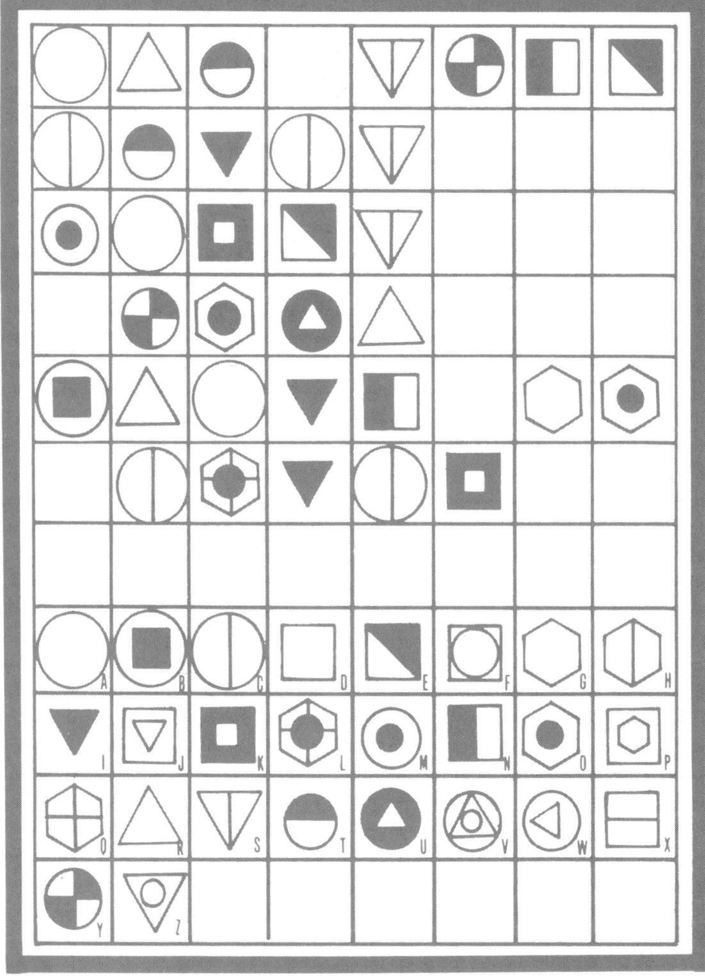


100. The Art Cryptogram offers opportunities to explore and invent unique design ciphers.

## 3-11 / Art Cryptogram

**Concept:** Creating design ciphers. A cryptogram is a communication in cipher; every letter is encoded by a corresponding symbol.

**Do:** 1. Using a draftsman's plastic template that has circles, triangles, squares, and other geometric shapes, invent a symbol for each letter of the alphabet by overlapping various combinations of the geometric forms. (Use handmade cardboard templates for making larger compositions.)

2. Select a well-known quotation or poem as the subject for making a cryptogram composition.

3. Use felt-tip pens to render the composition.

4. Exchange codes and messages with classmates or friends.

## 3-12 / Designs from Signs

**Concept:** Using graphic signs as a basis for abstraction.

**Do:** 1. Research calligraphy, foreign and ancient monograms, letter forms, and alphabets.

2. From some of the selected ciphers, make a series of abstracted designs.

3. Create a design, painting, or three-dimensional structure from the studies.

**101. Extructura Blanca** by Enrique Climent, 1964, Oil on canvas. Courtesy the artist.

**below: 102. Self-box** by George Pappas, mixed media. Courtesy the artist.

**below: 103. Symbolic Hands** by Mila Dudinsky, 1980, 18" (45.7 cm) high. Courtesy the artist. Surgical gloves, filled with soft fabric, take on symbolic overtones as they grapple with and attempt to break out of the bag.

## 3-13 / Symbolic Hands

**Concept:** Creating a sign-language tableau.

**Do:** 1. Obtain a package of plastic gloves from a local drugstore or medical-supply house.

2. Stuff them with fiberfill, chopped polyurethane, cloth, or cotton (obtainable from fabric stores).

3. Arrange the fingers and hands in symbolic gestures to narrate an idea or story, or have the hands hold a special object that evokes a symbolic idea.

4. Place the hands on a base or special environment such as a paper bag, box, bottle, mechanical device, et cetera.

## 3-14 / Emotion Box

**Concept:** Using found objects to symbolize emotions.

**Do:** 1. Find a box that has many compartments — a spice box, plastic sewing box, egg carton — or make a shallow compartmentalized box of cardboard.

2. Within each compartment, carefully arrange fragments of objects or images, textures, found objects, parts of mechanical devices, prose, poetry, calligraphy, and so on. Alter or combine the elements within each compartment to signify an emotional state or human quality. For example, a twisted ribbon might signify laziness; pieces of broken mirror glued over a photographic image might signify anxiety; a blue color field with cotton tufts might signify peacefulness; a mousetrap with a snared self-portrait could signify defeat; a piece of driftwood stuck with rusted nails might signify pollution, and so on.

3. Title each compartment.

**104. Big Mary** by Ramona Audley, 1980. Courtesy the artist. The fiber sculpture is made of cotton stockings and polyester fiberfill for the body, wig for the hair, painted wooden beads for the eyes, suture thread for creating teeth, and adult clothing, altered to fit.

## 3-15 / Stuffed, Stitched, and Sewn

**Concept:** Creating a Soft Sculpture Figure.

**Do:** Make a life-size character. Select a theme to portray.

1. Gather materials you'll need: Nylon hosiery, Fiberfill, flesh-tone thread, needle, scissors, scrap materials, and special accessories to finish the character.
2. Start by filling the hosiery with Fiberfill. Pinch, gather, and sew the surface to create anatomical features — eyes, nose, ears, mouth, etc. Use the same technique to create wrinkles, puckered faces, and finer anatomical details.
3. Use acrylic paint for painting lips, details. Sew or glue on buttons, beads, or taxidermy eyes; add accessories such as eyeglasses, hair, eyebrows, eyelashes, hat, clothing, gloves, shoes, etc. (Hands can be made by stuffing gloves with Fiberfill.)

**105. Spaghetti and Square Meatballs for C. Columbus, circa 1490,** by James Allison, 1979, Mixed media. Courtesy the artist.

**left: 106. Name Totem** by Joan Bailey, mixed media. Courtesy the artist.

## 3-16 / Name Totem

**Concept:** Creating a sculpture from letters.

**Do:** 1. Stylize the letters of your name, varying the design and shape of each letter.

2. Trace each letter to a slab of 1" (2.5 cm) styrofoam and cut out with knife or hacksaw blade (wrap masking tape around one end of the hacksaw blade to make a handle).

3. Decorate each letter in a different manner.

4. Stack the letters vertically to form a totem. Glue together with styrofoam cement.

## 3-17 / Look Who's Coming to Dinner

**Concept:** Creating a fantasy-dinner place setting.

**Do:** 1. Plan an imaginary dinner party. Invite a Hollywood celebrity, a historical character, a fictional character, or a local celebrity. What kind of dinner would you cook for each of the following: Joe DiMaggio, Sherlock Holmes, Count Dracula, O.J. Simpson, Mae West, Casanova, Vincent Van Gogh, Bella Lugosi, Piet Mondrian, René Magritte, Salomé, Charlie Chaplin, Sigmund Freud, Hieronymus Bosch, Cleopatra, Eve, The Lone Ranger, Johann Gutenberg.

2. Select a dinner guest from the list above or one of your own choosing. Let your imagination dictate an outrageous menu.

3. Fashion this "dinner" on a cardboard plate, using whatever materials are required to create it — Styrofoam, paper, yarn, cellophane, ping-pong balls, sand, glitter, found objects, paint, gesso, plaster, Polyfilla, wire, mosaic materials, and so on.

4. Serve the dinner on a long table. Use a 12" x 18" (30 x 45 cm) sheet of colored construction paper as a place setting. Provide a name card, napkin, and plastic cutlery as well.

5. Each member of the class should contribute his or her own special place setting to complete the dinner party.

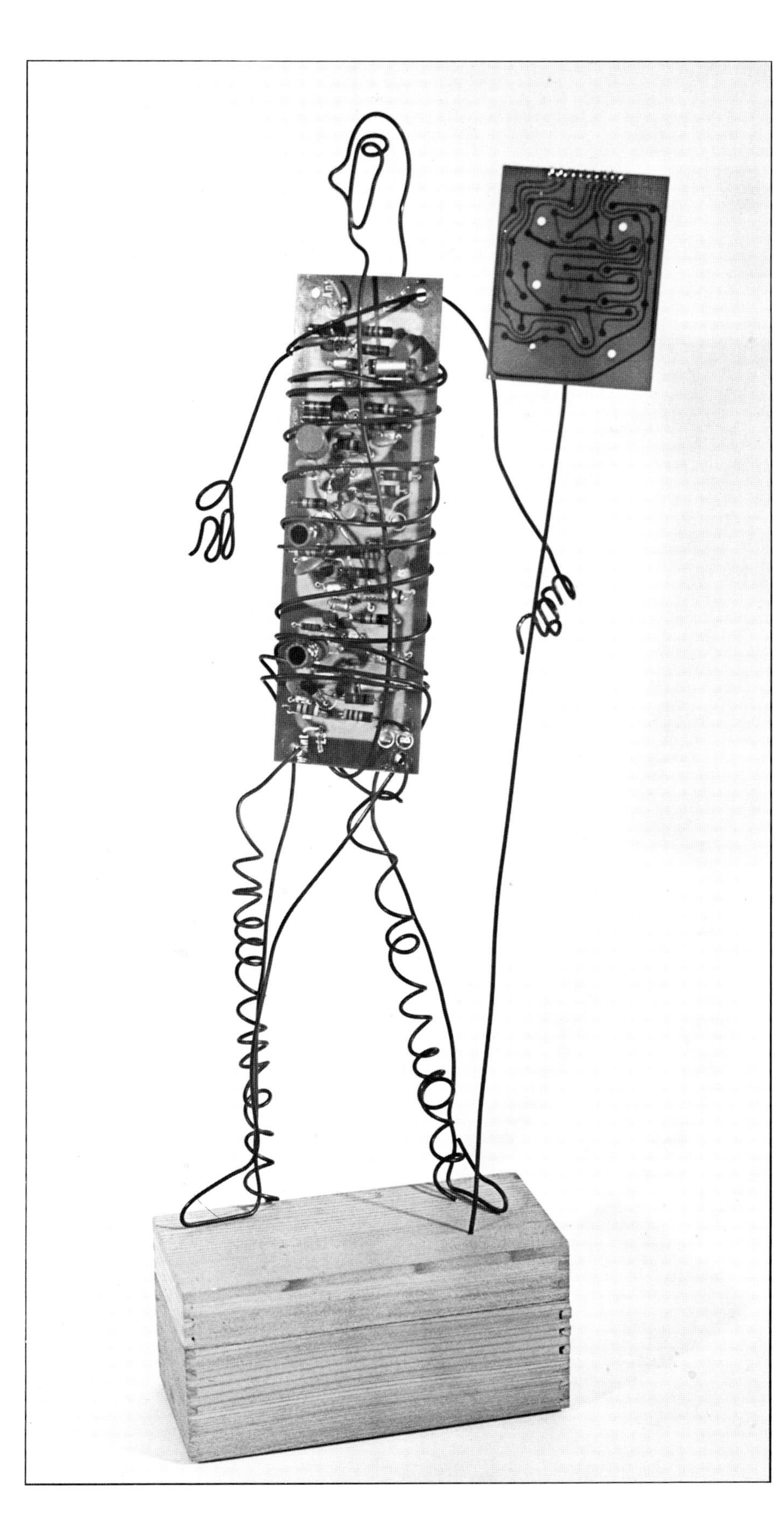

## 3-18 / Image of Man

**Concept:** Making a symbolic wire sculpture.

**Do:** 1. Portray a particular image of man: Man the Inventor, the Artist, the Sportsman, the Magician, the Hunter, and so on.

2. Interpret the concept with wire. Use any type (or types) of flexible wire to create a three-dimensional sculpture. Add additional elements to further emphasize the theme: clock parts, transistors, pills, ruler, map, mechanical parts, et cetera.

3. Mount the wire sculpture on a wood base and title appropriately.

## 3-19 / Image/Caption Switch

**Concept:** Creating new symbolic inferences by switching images and photo captions.

**Do:** 1. Cut out selected photographs from newspapers and magazines.

2. Also cut out the accompanying caption, along with captions and headlines from other articles that are completely unrelated.

3. Mix and match: paste the new headlines or captions under the photos to create new symbolic inferences.

**107. Technologic Vision** by Raymond Karpuzzi, mixed media. Courtesy the artist.

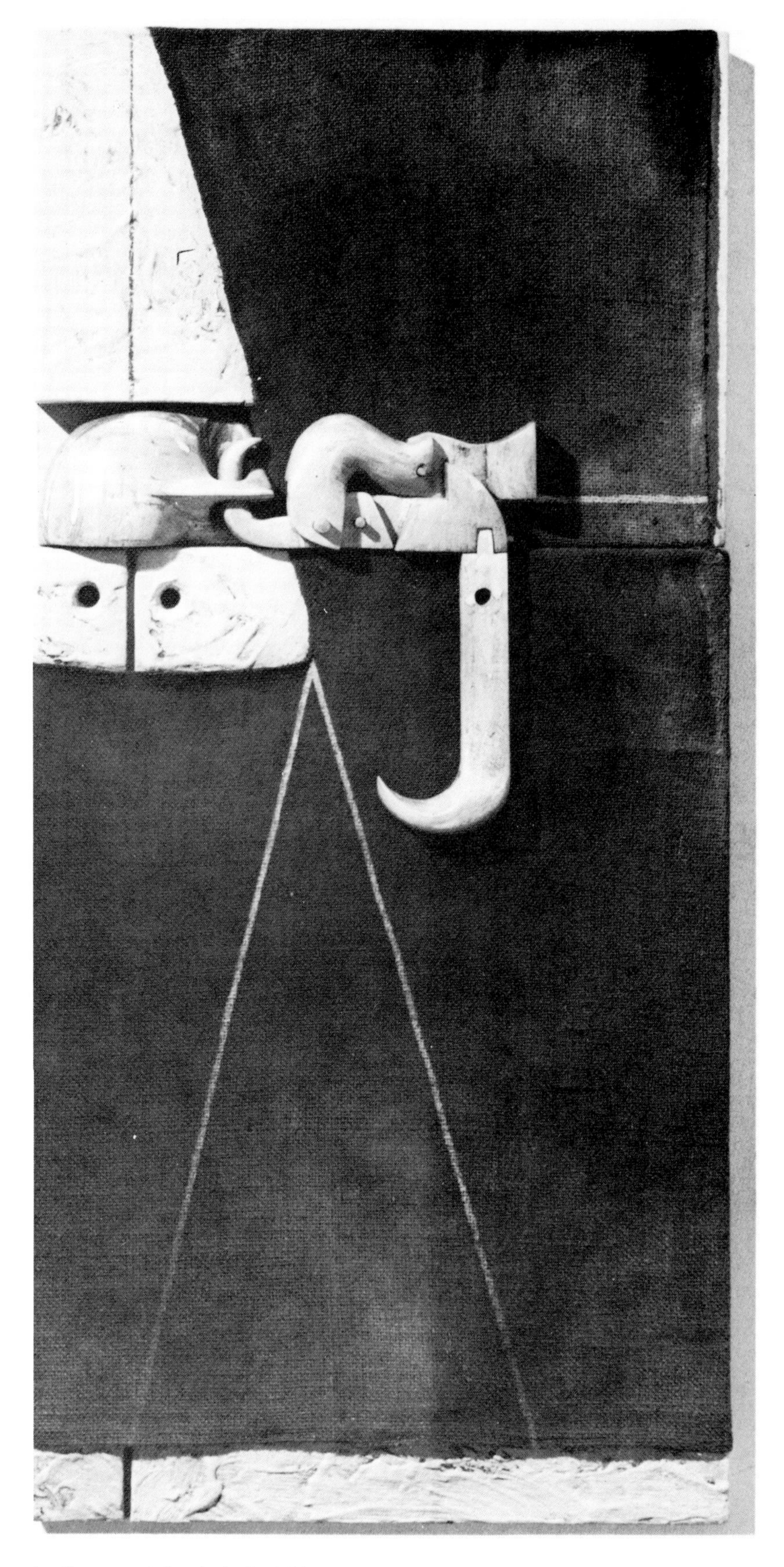

## 3-20 / Symbolic Abstraction

**Concept:** Creating abstract art from subjective stimulation.

**Do:** 1. Select a title for an art form that emanates from dream imagery or vivid recollection of a story or happening.

2. Without using representational imagery (figures, faces, et cetera), create an abstract composition that conveys feelings and emotions regarding the subject.

3. Used mixed media to make a bas relief assemblage.

**108. Trap for a Nightmare** by Bonevardi, 1973, 37" x 18" (94 x 45.7 cm), mixed media. Courtesy Galeria Bonino, New York.

CHAPTER 4

# MYTH AND MYTHMAKING

*The message of the myth is conveyed by the amalgam of its relationships and its mediations.*
Claude Levi-Strauss

Myths may function in one of several modes: (1) the *narrative,* wherein stories are created from the realm of pure fantasy and are told primarily to entertain; (2) the *operative,* the telling of stories for purposes of validating beliefs or enacting ritual ceremony; (3) the *speculative,* telling tales concerning life origins or functions. Traditionally, mythology comprises a special body of stories concerning the gods, demigods, and legendary heroes of a culture. Myths, like dreams, are events occurring in a particular time and space. They generally express meaning in symbolic form, and their significance depends on the listener's ability to understand the "disguised messages" they convey.

**109. Jail for Butterfly Hunters** by Pedro Friedeberg, 1964, pen-and-ink drawing. Courtesy the artist.

**110. Mixtec-Zapotec Codex,** painting.
Courtesy Design and Decoration.

# The Functions of Myths

Most classical myths are *etiological* in form; that, is, invented primarily to explain some mysterious phenomenon, occurrence, belief, or custom. In this manner, myths have served and continue to serve as psychological conditioners — shaping the minds of people within a society according to that society's values. Thus, myths are powerful tools for controlling people's behavior, from infancy to old age.

Carl Jung determined that an important function of myth is to render intellectually and socially tolerable that which would otherwise be incoherent. Thus, as human knowledge increases, scientific and intellectual explanations tend to explode old myths. Curiously enough, myths never disappear; as old ones are discarded, new ones take their place — including many posing as scientific "fact."

Jung's theory regarding the unconscious created a great stir in the early 1900s. He hypothesized that everyone has both a personal as well as a "collective" unconscious. The personal unconscious, he concluded, is created by the individual's own personal experiences and sensory perceptions; the collective unconscious is inherited from society at large and is mutually shared by all members of that society. Furthermore, Jung argued, the collective unconscious is divided into "archetypes" (basic patterns and symbols), and myths are one form of archetype.

# Myths — True or False Stories?

The word *myth* is ambiguous in meaning. Webster's dictionary defines it as a fictitious narrative or false story. Yet, as defined by scholars such as Jakob Malinowski, myth is also used to denote an "absolute truth." Malinowski, the famous researcher of the Trobiand Islanders, wrote that myth in a primitive society is not a mere tale, but a *reality lived* . Thus, according to the latter definition, myths are beliefs and social constructions that offer insights into the lives and customs of the believers and provide meaning and reason for their various rituals and ceremonies.

# The evolution of Heroes and Anti-Heroes

An examination of myths offers a penetrating look into our personal and collective beliefs regarding the popular heroes and legendary characters of our culture — as well as the anti-heroes and villains. Today, larger-than-life characters are created and discarded with regularity by the electronic and print media. Our deposed "surrogate deities" include former (perhaps soon to be revived) heroes such as Marilyn Monroe, Humphrey Bogart, James Dean, Elvis Presley, The Beatles, John F. Kennedy, and Martin Luther King. Modern-day mythological figures such as these spawn powerful cult followings. Fictional heroes include Superman, Batman, Tarzan, Captain America, James Bond (Agent 007), Wonder Woman, and The Bionic Man. Anti-heroes and "born losers" take the form of characters such as film stars Woody Allen and Peter Sellers, and cartoon characters Charlie Brown, Alfred E. Newman, Herman, and Ziggy.

From yesterday's folk tales to today's television "sit-coms," we extract our heroes and imbue them with superhuman qualities. This is the process of *mythicization.* We are all creatures of myth, maintaining old tales or restructuring them to suit our convenience. More often than not, however, myths appear as new structures that are reintegrated into our consciousness. Joseph Campbell's comment is insightful: "The latest incarnation of Oedipus, the continued romance of beauty and the beast, stands this afternoon on the corner of 42nd Street and Fifth Avenue, waiting for the light to change."

**111. Super Heroes** by Manuel Valdes and Rafael Solbes, 1972, 78-3/4" x 78-3/4" (200 x 200 cm), watercolor. Courtesy Galeria Juana Mordo, Madrid.

**left: 112. The Flying Foot: Racing Against the Storm** by Robert Graham, 1979, pen-and-ink drawing. Courtesy the artist.

# Personal Mythmaking

In a more contemporary sense, mythmaking denotes one's ability to generate any type of unique story — whether fictitious or not. As critic Lissie Borden stated, the personal myth can function as an outlet for eccentric imagery, self-discovery, religious confession, or as a spiritual experience. Science fiction and illustration are yet other forms of mythmaking, which concern themselves with bizarre fictionalizing: visitors from outer space, robots, androids, computer and machine intelligence, space travel, and galactic empires.

**below: 113. The Violence** by Guillermo Mesa, 1960, 39-1/2" x 63" (100.3 x 160 cm), oil on canvas. Courtesy the artist.

**114. Flying Shrouds** by Patti Warashina, 1978, 19" x 42" x 24" (48.3 x 106.9 x 60 cm), ceramic. Courtesy the artist.

**115. The Rialto** by Dana Boussard, 1971, 14' x 9' x 5' (4.3 x 2.7 x 1.5 m), velvet, fur, canvas, metal, stitchery, appliqué. Courtesy American Craft Museum, New York. Photo: Bobby Hanson.

**116. The Tower of Babel** by Pieter Brueghel, 1563, 44-7/8" (113.9 cm) high, oil on panel. Courtesy Kunsthistorisches Museum, Vienna.

**below: 117. People Who Live in a Circle** (detail) by Charles Simonds, 1972, clay and mixed media. Courtesy the artist. Photo: Rudolph Burckhardt. Miniature environments depicting imaginary civilizations are created by the artist and placed in outdoor settings such as cornices, doorways, and gutters.

**left: 118. Priests from the Order of the Hexagonal Orange** (detail) by Pedro Friedeberg, 1963, pen-and-ink drawing. Courtesy the artist.

**above: 119. Paladin Charge,** ©Roger Dean 1972, design for record-album cover. From *Views,* published by Dragon's Dream. Courtesy the artist.

**above: 120. Preferred Transition** by Deborah Horrell, 1981, 14" x 27" x 13" (35.6 x 68.6 x 30.5 cm), porcelain and graphite. Courtesy the artist. Slip cast bones and pencil drawings on paper-thin sheets of porcelain symbolize ephemeral and fragile qualities of life. The artist effectively combines both two- and three-dimensional media within this metaphorical composition.

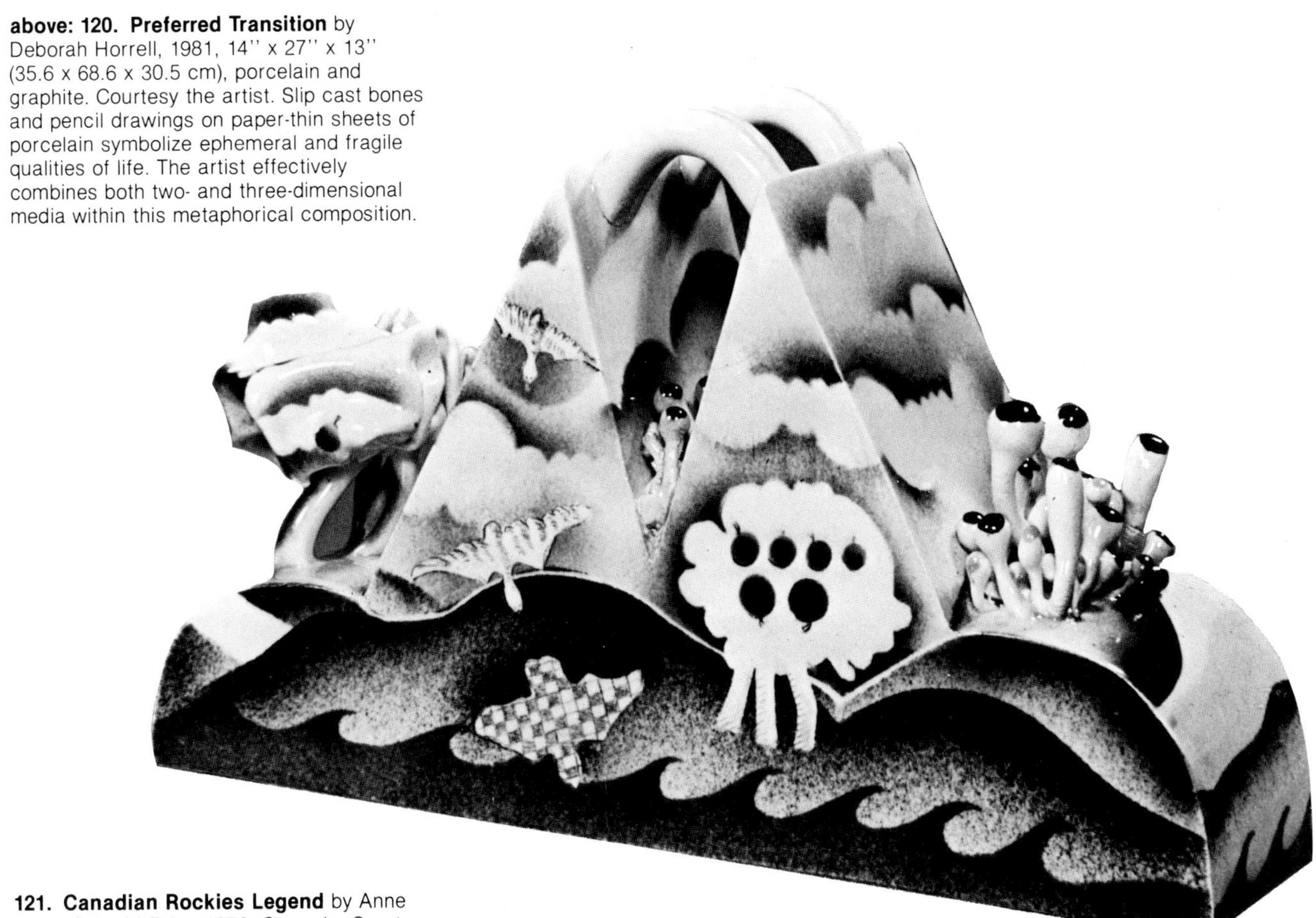

**121. Canadian Rockies Legend** by Anne Marie Schmid Esler, 1979, Ceramic. Courtesy the artist.

**right: 122. Asessippi Night Mask** by Don Proch, 1974, 12" x 12" x 12" (30.5 x 30.5 x 30.5 cm), mixed media, drawing on fiberglass. Photo: Ernest Mayer.

**below: 123. Vegetable Nightclub** by Marvin Jones, 16" x 18" (40.6 x 45.7 cm), etching. Courtesy the artist. An impossible scenario: vegetables "stepping out" - enjoying dinner, wine, and a nightclub review.

# 4

## ACTIVITIES

### 4-1 / Reinterpreting Ancient Myths

**Concept:** Creating personal versions of ancient myths.

**Do:** 1. Select an interesting story or legend from ancient mythology.

2. Invent your own characters to serve as substitutes for the original characters. (Use animals, modern-day media heroes, cartoon characters, plants, animated devices, et cetera.)

3. Render your idea in clay. Make a ceramic sculpture, bisque fire, and decorate with acrylic paint.

### 4-2 / Impossible Scenarios

**Concept:** Stimulating imaginative fantasy.

**Do:** 1. Can you visualize the following situations? Create a dialogue for them.

(a) Old shoes are waiting for repair in a cobbler's shop. What do they have to say when the cobbler isn't around?

(b) Cigarette butts in an ash tray have a conversation after a party. What do they say?

(c) Wrecked autos in a junk yard talk to each other. What do they say?

(d) An artist leaves his studio for a coffee break. While he is gone, the brushes, paints, canvas, and shop tools in his studio start a conversation. What do they say?

2. Make up your own list of five additional scenarios and write a dialogue for each.

3. Make a drawing or cartoon of one of the scenarios.

**124. Frog Noah** by David Gilhooly, 1976, 19" x 16" (48.3 x 40.6 cm), glazed ceramic. Courtesy Hansen Fuller Goldeen Gallery, San Francisco. Through his selected emissary (the frog), the artist reconstructs events in world history, altering them as he pleases to provide scenarios for his "frog kingdom."

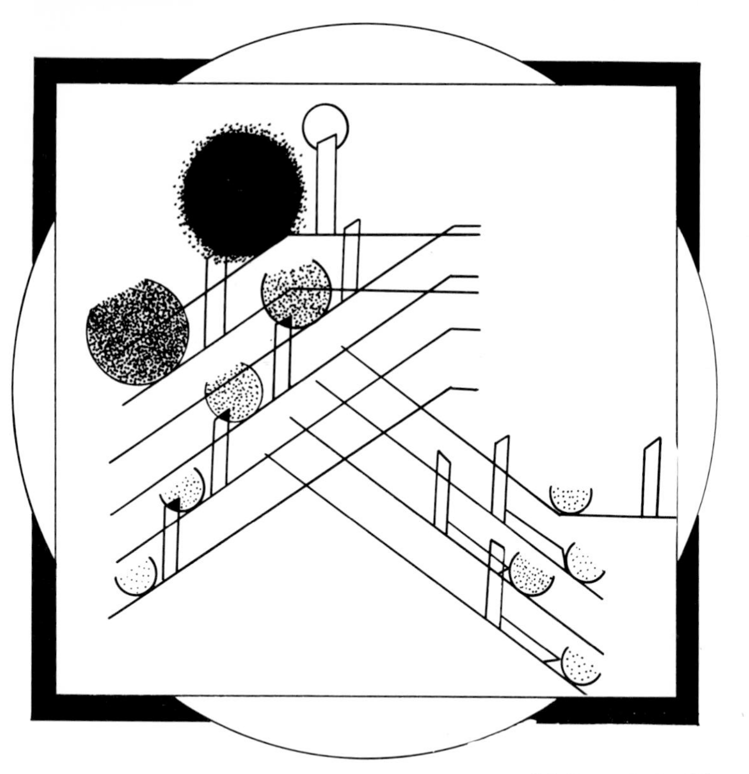

**125. A Bao A Qu** by Jan Facey, 1980, pen-and-ink drawing. A visual interpretation of Jorge Luis Borges's story.

## 4-3 / A Bao A Qu

**Concept:** Visualizing a mythological event in graphic form.

**Do:** 1. Read the following story by Jorge Luis Borges, "A Bao A Qu."

2. Interpret the story by making a drawing, painting, or three-dimensional structure.

### "A Bao A Qu" by Jorge Luis Borges

If you want to look out over the loveliest landscape in the world, you must climb to the top of the Tower of Victory in Chitor. There, standing on a circular terrace, one has a sweep of the whole horizon. A winding stairway gives access to this terrace, but only those who do not believe in the legend dare climb up. The tale runs:

On the stairway of the Tower of Victory there has lived since the beginning of time a being sensitive to the many shades of the human soul and known as the A Bao A Qu. It lies dormant, for the most part on the first step, until at the approach of a person some secret life is touched off in it, and deep within the creature an inner light begins to glow. At the same time, its body and almost translucent skin begins to stir. But only when someone starts up the spiralling stairs is the A Bao A Qu brought to consciousness, and then it sticks close to the visitor's heels, keeping to the outside of the turning steps, where they are most worn by the generations of pilgrims. At each level the creature's color become more intense, its shape approaches perfection, and the bluish form it gives off is more brilliant. But it achieves its ultimate form only at the topmost step, when the climber is a person who has attained Nirvana and whose acts cast no shadows. Otherwise, the A Bao A Qu hangs back before reaching the top, as if paralysed, its body incomplete, its blue growing paler, and its glow hesitant. The creature suffers when it cannot come to completion, and its moan is a barely audible sound, something like the rustling of silk. Its span of life is brief, since as soon as the traveller climbs down, the A Bao A Qu wheels and tumbles to the first steps, where, worn out and almost shapeless, it waits for the next visitor. People say that its tentacles are visible only when it reaches the middle of the staircase. It is also said that it can see with its whole body and that to the touch it is like the skin of a peach.

In the course of centuries, the A Bao A Qu has reached the terrace only once.

**right: 126. Box #89** by Lucas Samaras, 1974, 14-1/2" x 19" x 17" (36.8 x 48.3 x 43.2 cm), mixed media. Courtesy Pace Gallery, New York. Photo: Al Mozell. Using the box format, the artist creates a tangible yet cryptic personal mythology. Selected fragments, images, pins, beads, tiles, and shells are combined in a free use of mixed media. What emotions does it arouse?

**below: 127.** As in George Orwell's *Animal Farm,* these normally docile farm animals suddenly turn on their keepers.

## 4-4 / Fantasy Case

**Concept:** Portraying the alter ego or "other self" in three-dimensional form.

**Do:** 1. Within the interior space of a plastic or wooden box, arrange various objects, photographic images, drawings, poems, mementos, souvenirs, and memorabilia that portray your alter ego or the alter ego of a well-known contemporary or historical personality.

## 4-5 / Revolt

**Concept:** Creating a mythological event.

**Do:** 1. Think up a story involving the imaginary revolt of domestic animals, computers, machines, kitchen appliances, elevators, flowers, and so on.

2. Visualize your idea by making a drawing.

## 4-6 / Magic Machine

**Concept:** Inventing mythological devices, magic machines.

**Do:** 1. Make some sketches that describe it in graphic form. Examples: The Cloud-Making Machine, The Pollution Eliminator, The Straw-to-Gold Converter, The Rainbow Catcher, The Rainmaker.

2. Realize the device in three-dimensional form. Make a model with cardboard, wood, fabric, and mixed media.

3. Create a "tech manual" or pictorial diagram that describes the intricacies of the device and how it functions.

## 4-7 / Fantastic Transport

**Concept:** Inventing an outrageous mode of transport.

**Do:** 1. Think up a utopian form of transport involving either human, animal, or imaginary characters.

2. Visualize the idea by making a drawing.

3. Visualize the idea by making a three-dimensional structure.

**128. Cloud Box** by Sylvia Palchinski, 1970, 12' (3.7 cm) high, flexible plastic, stuffing. Courtesy Glenbow-Alberta Institute, Calgary, Alberta, Canada.

**129. Fantastic Travel** by Grandville, pen and ink drawing.

**left: 130. Uncle** by Robert Arneson, 1978, 40" x 19" x 19" (101.6 x 48.3 x 48.3 cm), glazed ceramic. Courtesy Allan Frumkin Gallery, New York.

**below: 131. Darby Street** by Michael Garman, mixed media. Courtesy the artist. Combining sculpture, painting, and collage, the artist has created a diorama depicting the vicissitudes of life in the inner-city slums.

## 4-8 / Monument

**Concept:** Creating a visual tribute to a special hero.

**Do:** 1. Design an "outrageous" monument for an imaginary character: The World's Greatest Gossip, The World's Greatest Butterfly Collector, The World's Greatest Lover, The World's Greatest Contortionist, The World's Greatest High Jumper, The World's Greatest Artist. Add to the list yourself.

2. Realize your idea three-dimensionally: model it in pottery clay, bisque fire, and paint with acrylic; or use papier-mâché and tempera paint.

## 4-9 / Street Myth

**Concept:** Creating a bas-relief or tableau of a building façade.

**Do:** 1. Using clay or papier-mâché, construct a bas-relief or tableau depicting the front of a building from a metropolitan setting: the front of an old hotel, bar, grocery store, hamburger stand, drugstore, pool hall, popcorn stand, newspaper kiosk, movie house, dance hall, et cetera.

2. Add the required details, props, or figures; paint with acrylic.

**132. Necromicon** by H.R. Gieger, 1976, 27-1/2" x 39-1/4" (70 x 100 cm). Courtesy the artist.

## 4-10 / Science Fiction Art

**Concept:** Creating images and legends from science-fiction motifs.

**Do:** 1. Select a theme from the list below:

- Spacecraft Design
- Space Colonies
- Space Environments
- Space Warfare
- Galactic Nightmares and Cataclysms
- Galactic Utopias
- Computer and Machine Intelligence
- Robots and Androids
- Mutants and Hybrids
- Space-Time Travel
- Survival Systems
- Space Games
- Cosmic Courtship
- Bionics

2. Develop a drawing, painting, or three-dimensional structure based on the selected theme.

## 4-11 / Tower

**Concept:** Reinterpreting an ancient legend.

**Do:** 1. Contemplate Brueghel's *Tower of Babel* (see page 79)

2. Create a modern-day version of the tower.

3. Use a medium of your choice: drawing, cartoon, photo-collage, clay, or a three-dimensional construction.

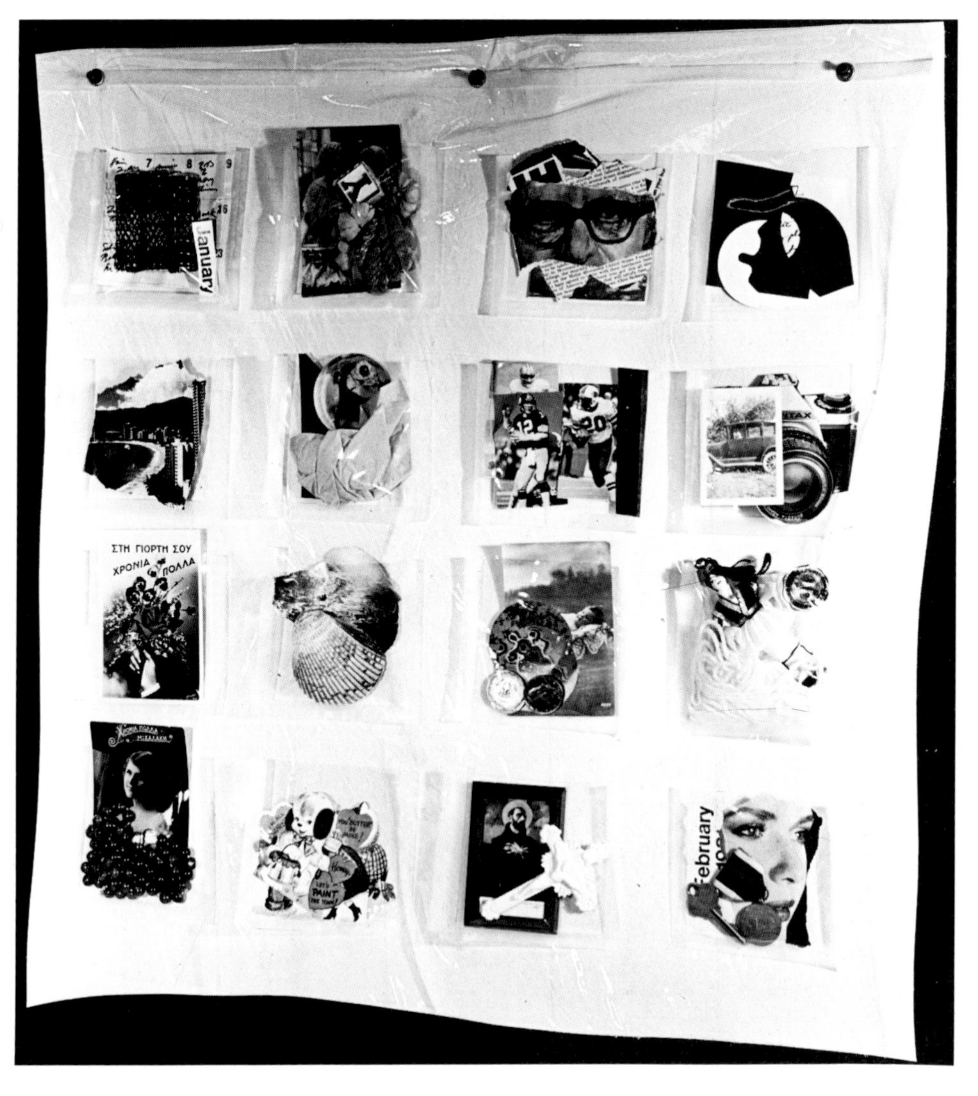


**133. Diary** by Vivien Ralston, mixed media. Courtesy the artist.

**below: 134.** Motivating creativity through the invention of fantasy machines.

## 4-12 / Diary

**Concept:** Creating a pictorial diary.

**Do:** 1. Cut a sheet of clear polyethylene or cheesecloth to 4' x 4' (1.2 x 1.2 m) in size.

2. Cut out 16 additional pieces of plastic that measure 10" (25.4 cm) square to act as pockets.

3. Use freezer tape to affix the pockets to the large sheet of plastic. (Make four rows, each having four pockets.)

4. Stuff objects, letters, graphics, poetry, tickets, photographs, designs, drawings, yarn or loose fabric, toys, or other souvenirs and memorabilia into the pockets.

5. Set two grommets in the upper corners of the plastic and hang it up.

## 4-13 / Utopian Inventions

**Concept:** Creating inventions that will never become realities.

**Do:** 1. Make up a list of inventions that would enrich our lives but would be impossible to realize. Examples:

*An Animal Talk Translator.* A mechanical device that decodes animal sounds so humans can understand them.

*Finding Machine.* A device that locates lost articles.

*Book Digester.* A device that clamps on your head and allows you to digest the contents of books without having to read them.

*Self-Analysis Machine.* A gadget that tells you what your problem is and what to do about it.

*Smallifying Machine.* A device that makes people small in order to explore small places.

*The Ultimate Weapon.* A weapon of warfare so gruesome to contemplate that war would be outlawed forever.

2. Visualize your invention by making a sketch, either in the form of a drawing for the patent office, a mechanical drawing, or a freehand rendering.

3. Use mixed media to make a three-dimensional model.

## 4-14 / Reconstructions

**Concept:** "Re-doing" an old masterpiece.

**Do:** 1. Select a painting, sculpture, or well known image from art history for interpretation.

2. Re-do the work: up-date it, change colors, media, characters, et cetera.

## 4-15 / Mythological Beast

**Concept:** Discovering the skeleton of a mythological creature. (Pseudo archeology)

**Do:** 1. Select a theme based on a mythological character or legendary beast: Big Foot, The Lochness Monster, Cyclops, Cyborg, The Troll, Bionic Beast, et cetera.

2. Using pottery clay, fashion a skull, skeleton, or anatomical fragment of the legendary creature.

3. Place the "evidence" in a display box; label accordingly.

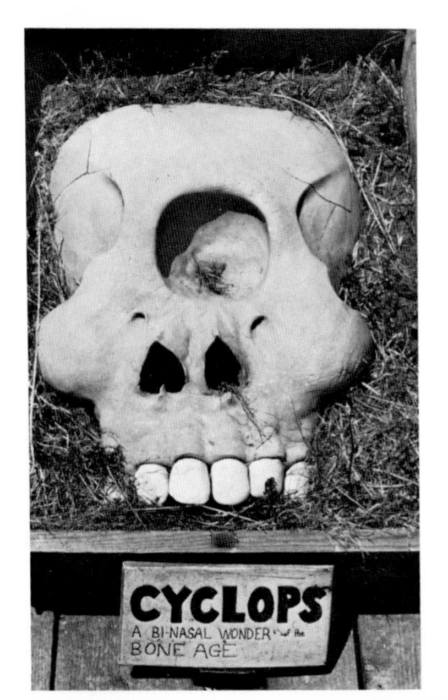


**above: 135. Woman in a Landscape** by Paul Wunderlich, 1976, 22-3/4" x 20-1/2" (22.8 x 20.4 cm), oil and tusche on paper. Courtesy the artist.

**left: 136. Christina** by Bernard Langlais, 1970, 7' (2.1 m) high, wood. Courtesy the artist. This work is a three-dimensional "reconstruction" of Andrew Wyeth's famous painting by the same name.

**left: 137. Cyclops, the Bi-Nasal Wonder of the Bone Age** by Clayton Bailey, 22" x 31-1/2" (55.9 x 80 cm), clay. Courtesy the artist. Using imagination (and poetic license), the artist has unearthed a "heraldic find", the skull of the legendary one-eyed giant; artifacts and documentation serve as "proof of discovery."

**138. Spectre over San Francisco** by Nicholas Roukes, 1980, photographic collage.

## 4-16 / Architectural Fantasy

**Concept:** Creating an architectural myth with photo-montage.

**Do:** 1. Collect photographs of city skylines, landscapes, and seascapes.

2. Also collect photos of household and technical objects: egg beater, toothbrush, toaster, electric fan, automobile grill, et cetera.

3. Carefully implant the photo of the technical gadget within the photo of the environment to create a surreal cityscape or landscape. Examples: a giant toothbrush towering above the Empire State Building, an egg beater projecting from the San Francisco skyline, a 1937 Packard grill implanted within the skyline of Chicago.

## 4-17 / Psychological Map of the City

**Concept:** Portraying the psychological or emotional state of a city.

**Do:** 1. From every section of your local newspaper, cut out photographs, illustrations, headlines and fragments of copy.

2. Paste all of the elements together on a sheet of drawing paper to make a collage — the psychological map of your city.

**139. View of Calgary from the Bow** by Joseph Della Maggiore, 1979, photomontage. Courtesy the artist.

**right: 140. Toadster** by Heather Hemphill, 1980, soft sculpture. Courtesy Alberta Culture, Edmonton. What else but raisinfly bread would you toast in a toadster?

## 4-18 / Crosslinks

**Concept:** Creating preposterous hybrids.

**Do:** 1. Make up a list of mythological hybrids that are inspired by crosslinks. Example: What do you get when you cross an *automobile* with an *alligator?* Sample response: a *carrigator.*

2. Visualize a crosslink by making a cartoon, drawing, ceramic sculpture, or soft sculpture.

3. Make up your own crosslinks. What do you get when you cross a __________ with a __________?

**below: 141. Notebook for a Crucifixion** by Sandra Jackman, 1980, 12-1/4" x 9-1/4" x 7-1/4" (31.1 x 23.5 x 18.4 cm), mixed media. Courtesy the artist.

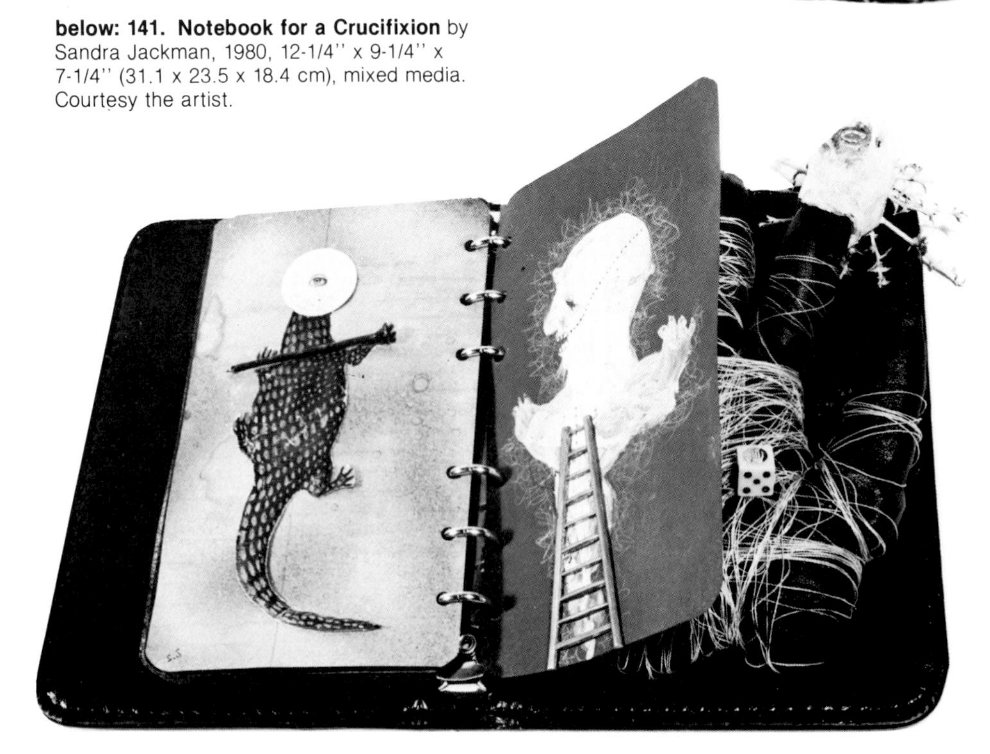

## 4-19 / Fantasy Book

**Concept:** Making a nonverbal book.

**Do:** 1. Use a 3" (7.5 cm) wide ring binder to serve as the cover and spine for the book.

2. Cut out three to five pieces of cardboard to serve as pages. Punch holes to accommodate the binder rings.

3. Select a title for your book based on an emotion: *The Fear Book, The Happy Book, The Mellow Book,* and so on.

4. Use mixed media to render the designs on each page (incorporate both two- and three-dimensional components such as photographs, relatively flat objects, yarn, string, collage papers, drawings. Design a cover for the book.

CHAPTER 5

# RITUAL, GAME, AND PERFORMANCE

*The association of myths and rituals in certain social conditions is due to the propensity of men, especially in uninhibited and savage societies, for acting out any event or description whatever, whether real or fictitious.* G.S. Kirk

## Ritual

Ritual and ceremony are among the fundamental ways in which we impose order and pattern on human existence. Although the term "ritual" has been used primarily to designate forms of private or public worship or atonement, its more contemporary definition denotes any ceremonious action or behavior designated to be "acted out" in a prescribed way.

**Ritual and Social Conduct.** From the moment of birth, we are subjected to an endless number of rituals that train us to be "civilized," responsible members of society. Ritualistic behavior is innate in animals; in man, however, it is learned, impressed in the early formative years and constantly reinforced throughout life. Consequently, in human growth and development there is very little behavior that is not ritualistic in one form or another. In every realm of human existence — work, recreation, play, social action, love, worship, education, marriage, and death — there are particular social codes that dictate appropriate conduct. From the rigidly established behavioral demands of formal ceremonies to the more casual conduct demanded at parties and social functions, we are all creatures of ritual — seeking our roles, acting out our parts. A ritual is a special kind of game played out by rules like any other game that acts as a fundamental means of developing and maintaining a social system.

**142. Salmon Dance.** A performance event by Evelyn Roth and Hannalore, 1979. Photo: Hannalore. The Salmon consists of 600 multicolored segments of nylon fabric and measures 500 feet in length. Four participants costumed as the characters Frog, Raven, Eagle, and Bear emerge from the giant Salmon as eggs encapsulated within plastic bubbles. As they slowly rid themselves of their shells, they perform various ritual movements as they explore the environment, ultimately forming a "living totem." Human, another character, enters the scenario and is prepared by the other characters for "integration to their dance." Although awkward at first, Human ultimately learns to move in harmony with the other creatures.

**De-Ritualization.** Although restraints are imposed on our impulsive actions in terms of what is deemed socially acceptable, no restraints impinge on our creative imaginations. Here, the only restraints are those imposed by the limitations of creative fantasy. Through creative work, the artist "de-ritualizes" his real-life behavior and establishes a personal identity. In the make-believe world of the imagination, the artist can do that which in real life might result in either admonition, arrest, or consignment to a strait jacket. Marshal McLuhan, in *Understanding Media,* states that art became a "civilized substitute" for magic ritual and ceremony, the result of the "detribilization" that came with literacy.

## Games

Games are created and played for one purpose — for fun and diversion. They are defined as *contests* among adversaries that operate within a framework of rules that governs their attainment of a specified objective. A game generally involves opportunities for players to change elements of a controlled situation so that new patterns occur. These may challenge individual or collective skills involving mental strategy, physical or creative skills, or a combination of any or all of these. Elements of chance (dice, spinners, and so forth) may also be an integral part of a game.

**Differences Between Games and Pure Play.** Pure play is egocentric in nature, insofar as it is a spontaneous and intuitive form of creative behavior that evolves without benefit of preconceived rules. Children's play, for example, is a creative experience that amalgamates elements of the child's real world with a make-believe world of pure fantasy. Since play is extemporaneous in nature, it is not subject to replication as are games.

**143. Kachina Doll,** 18" (45.7 cm) high. Courtesy Glenbow Museum, Calgary, Alberta, Canada.

**144. Game in Layers #2** by Jim Melchert, 1968-69, 24" x 24" x 18-1/2" (61 x 61 x 47 cm), acrylic plastic and mixed media. Courtesy Obelisk Gallery, Boston. The participant can move the various elements of the sculpture to any position within its three planes, thus changing the character of the work.

**Designing Games.** Ten points to consider in designing games are drawn from Alice Kaplan Gordon's book, *Games for Growth*:

1. Define the game objectives.
2. Determine the scope of the game.
3. Determine the players.
4. Define the players' goals.
5. Determine the players' resources.
6. Determine the rules that govern action.
7. Determine interaction sequence among players.
8. Identify external constraints.
9. Decide scoring rules or winning criteria.
10. Determine tangible form — board games, field games, et cetera.

**Scores.** A score is a plan or guide for realizing any kind of creative work that is meant to be performed or executed at a later date. Musical notation, dance notation, dramatic scripts, architectural and engineering plans — all are forms of graphic scores. These are not art forms in their own right, but simply means of communicating information or directions to participants for the subsequent realization of the actual work itself.

Interdisciplinary art forms such as performance events, conceptual art, and kinetic art make use of graphic scores as a means of planning and staging the work. In a more mundane sense, cooking recipes, directions for assembling toys or tools, shopping lists, calendar notes, and traffic signs are also scores.

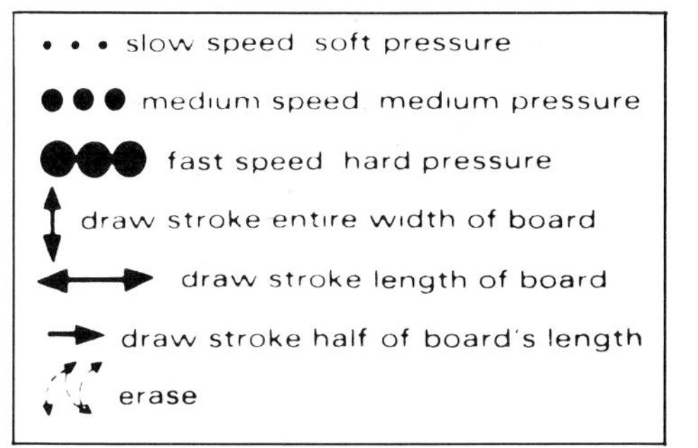


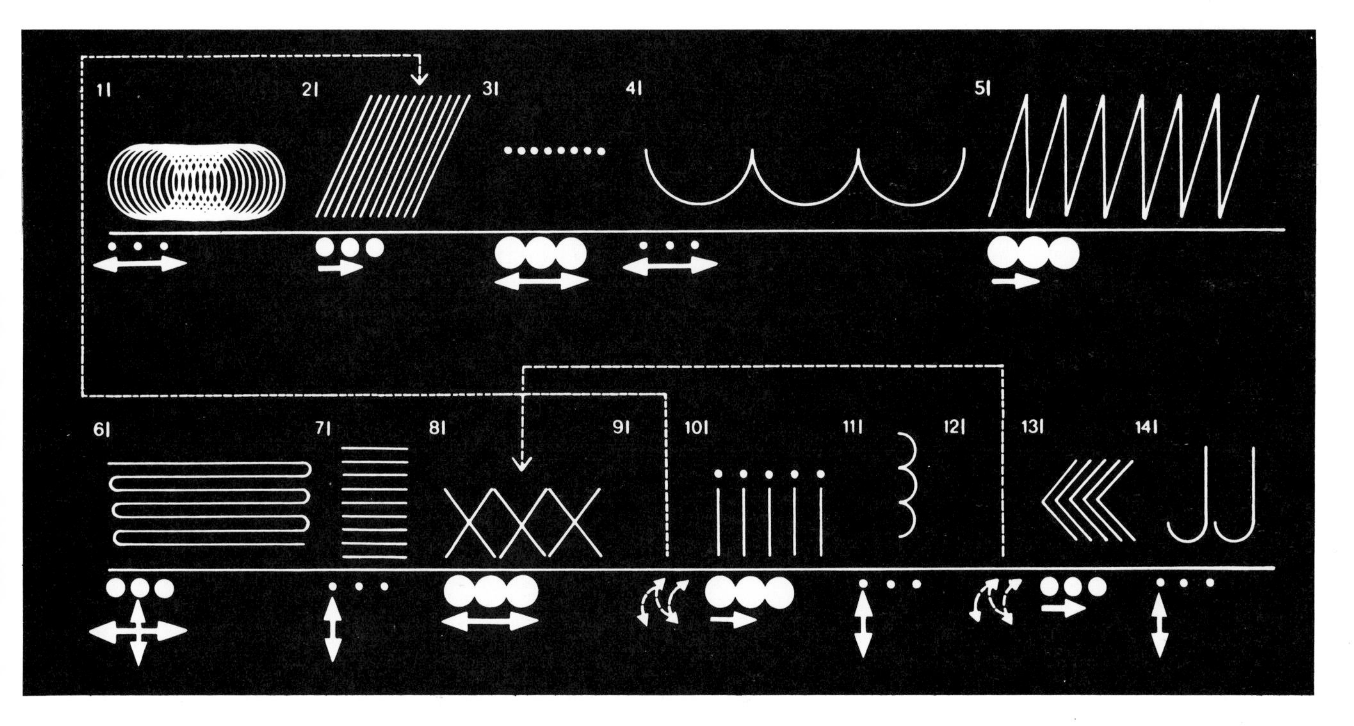


**145. Blackboard Event** by Tom Ockerse. A score performed by one person, using chalkboard, chalk, and eraser. Listeners are seated so they can hear but not see what is drawn on the chalkboard.

*Directions:* Reading each line from left to right, copy each type of stroke as it appears above each of the horizontal lines. Short vertical lines numbered in sequence mark the beginning of each stroke. All symbols appearing below the horizontal lines give information as to the speed and pressure of the strokes as well as the area they should cover. Length of performance approximately three minutes.

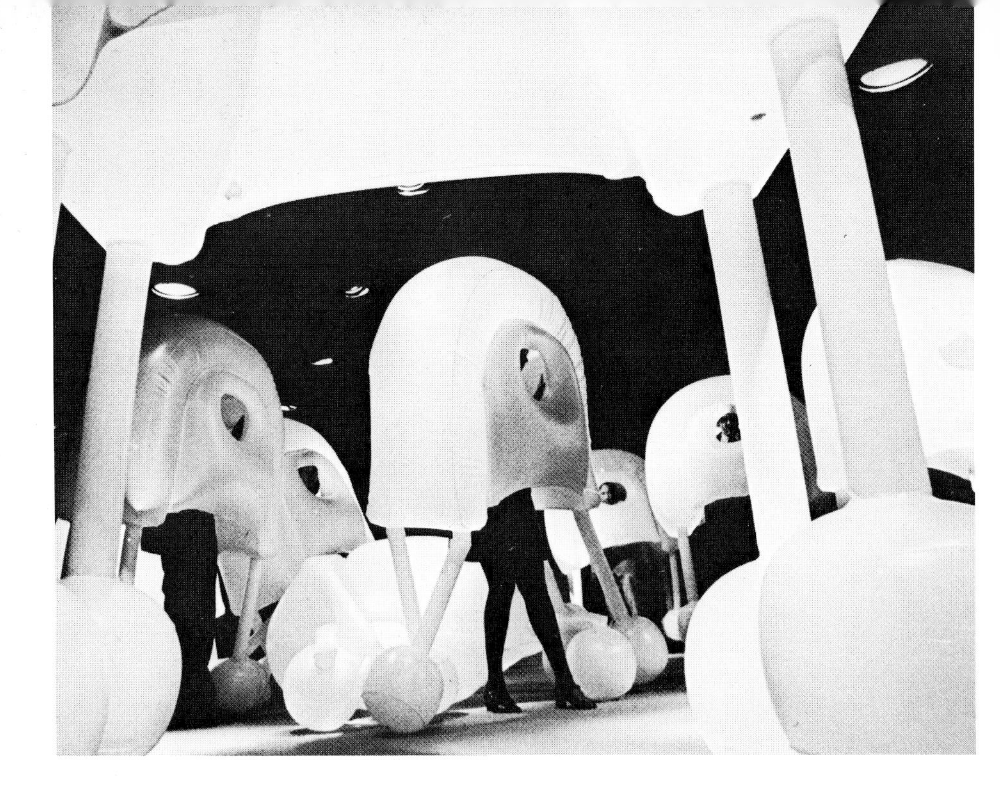

**146. Phosphorescent Inflatables** by Heidi and Carl Bucher, 1971, soft sculpture. Courtesy the artists.

# Performance

Performance art is also described as "live-art" or "action-art". This art form does not have a material nature in the way sculpture and painting do, it is not object-making but *action* that is central to its character. Ideas and concepts are communicated through live performances by artists using their bodies as an art medium. Also unlike the pictorial arts, which are exhibited in galleries apart from the artists, performance art provides a direct contact between artist and spectator. Although some performance pieces may be created in private and recorded on video tape for deferred performance, this art form is usually presented to a live audience for its strongest impact.

The current nature of performance art stems from a long history that includes early Dada, assemblage art, the Bauhaus of the 1920s, happenings of the '60s, and Surrealism, as well as aspects of theatre, parade, circus, ceremony, and ritual. Performance art is conceived in two basic stages: (1) the creation of the idea by the artist and its documentation in the form of a script or score, and (2) the interpretation and deployment of the piece by selected performers. Performance art is interdisciplinary insofar as it may combine aspects of sculpture, painting, drama, music, dance, and technology — often within the framework of a single piece.

Especially made costumes, "wearables," props, or backgrounds are often used, although ideas for performance pieces can be created with simple materials or commonplace elements. Events may involve spectator participation, interaction with nature, or the selection of unusual sites such as rooftops, beaches, or swimming pools as the setting for the event.

Chantal Pontbriand, a performance artist from Canada, describes her art as a process of "charging space with a presence." The spectator participates insofar as he may recognize that presence and find in it a sign of something with which he associates himself. Richard Foreman, another performance artist, states that the audience can savor the presentation only if it is prepared to establish new perceptual habits — habits that may be in conflict with established modes of thinking.

**147. Slat Dance** by Oscar Schlemmer, performed by Manda von Kreibig, Bauhaus Stage, 1927. Photo courtesy Staatsgalerie, Stuttgart.

**148. Twenty-Five Horsepower:** Performance event by Leopoldo Maler, 1980, Dublin, Ireland. Courtesy the artist. Dubbed a visual metaphor regarding the fiction of power. The artist supervised a parade of twenty-five horses and a twenty-five horsepower automobile through the front square of Trinity College in Dublin. Accompanying the parade was the repetitious drone of the artist's voice through loudspeakers: "Horsepower, art power, sun power, steam power, sea power, land power, gun power, power, power, power."

**left: 150. Plucked Undulation** by Frank Young, 1971, 17' x 3-1/2' (5.1 x 1.1 m), feathers, acrylic, vinyl, kinetics. Courtesy American Craft Museum, New York. A self contained kinetic construction, programmed to circulate goose feathers within its interior at one-minute intervals,

**below: 151. The Last Supper:** Tableau by Leopoldo Maler, 1972, 13 chairs, table, cloth, barbed wire, plastic lambs. Courtesy the artist. In comparing Leopoldo's version of the *Last Supper* to Da Vinci's, the spectator is forced to reassess the import of both images. What is the artist telling us in this contemporary version? "Sacrificial lambs", dangling from the ceiling, along with empty chairs and barbed wire, appear to portray man's quest for personal glut rather than sentiments of atonement.

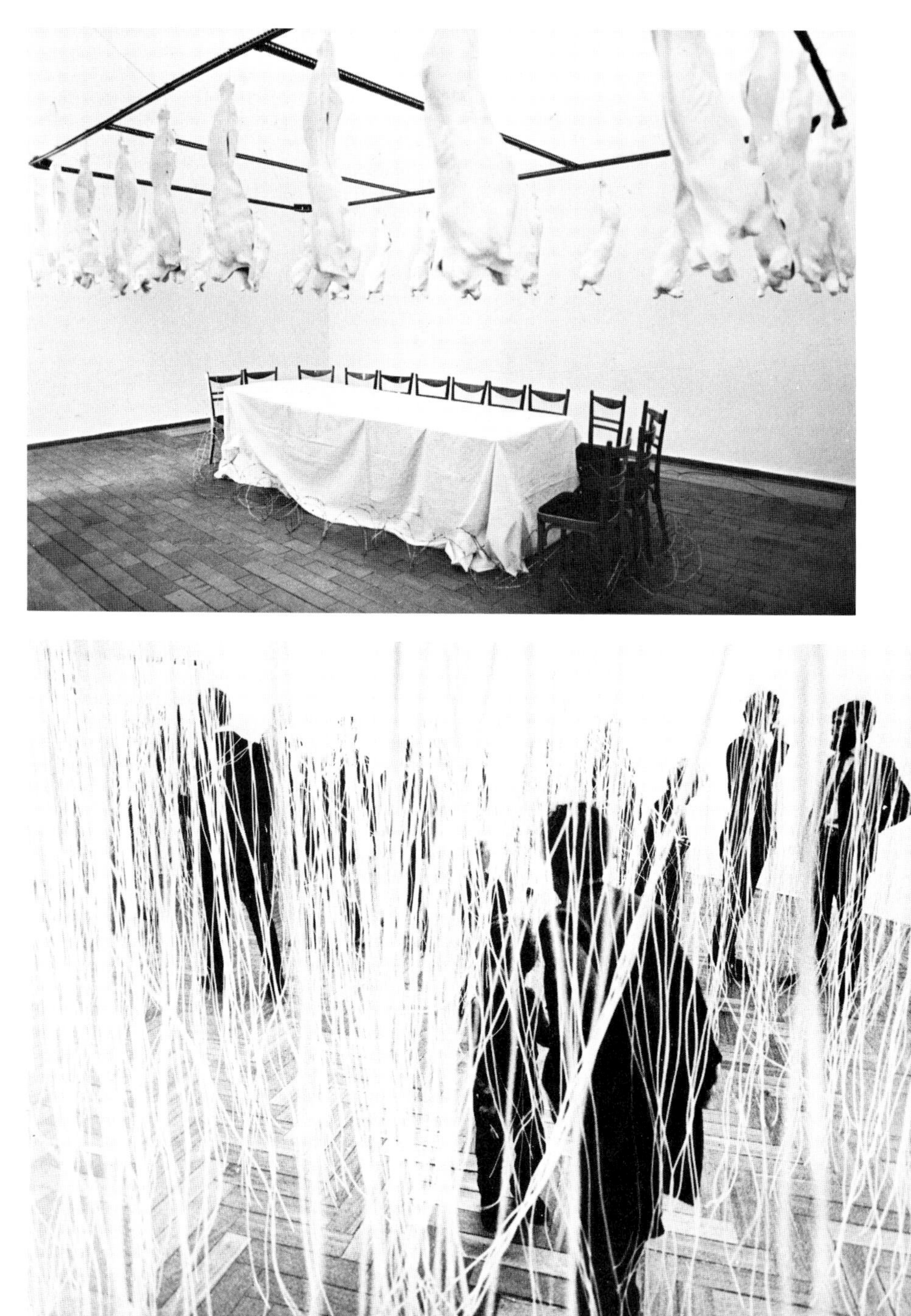

**right: 149. Pénétrable** by Raphael Soto, 1969, 13' x 26' x 26' (3.9 x 8 x 8 m). Courtesy Stedelijk Museum, Amsterdam. Photo: Ad Petersen.

**above: 152. Homage** by Leopoldo Maler, 1974, typewriter, gas burner. Courtesy the artist. An old typewriter, its roller replaced with a gas jet, becomes a metaphoric object.

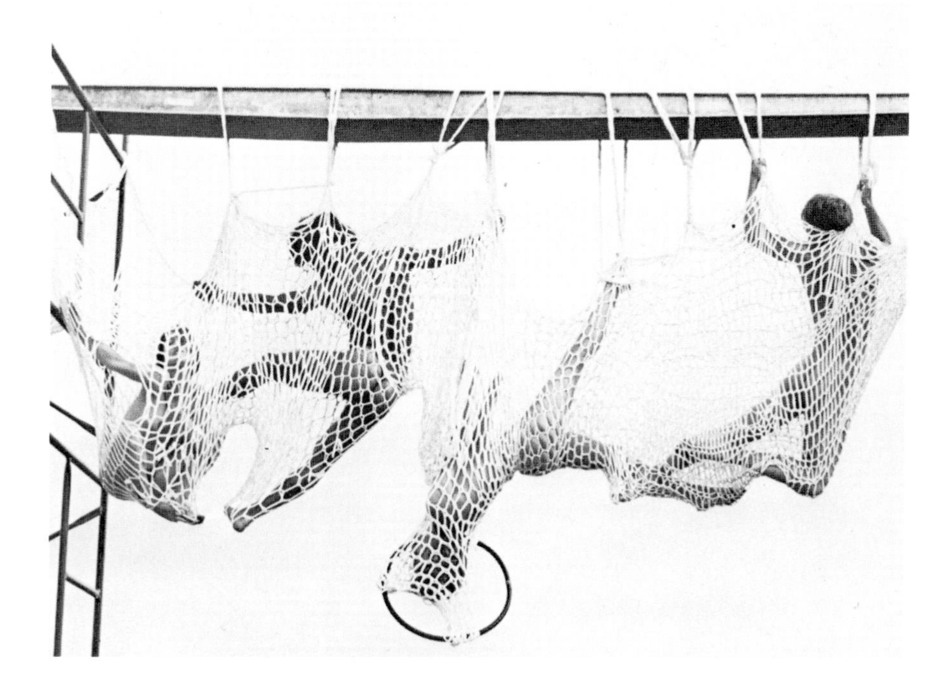

**right: 153. Possum Times:** performance event by Evelyn Roth and the Evelyn Roth Moving Sculpture Co. Courtesy the artist.

154. Portable video camera, video cassette recorder. Courtesy Sony Inc.

**Video.** Video is an *experiential* medium. It is performance-oriented — involving people doing things — and can document or communicate experiences that have intense personal qualities, as well as investigate aspects of structure and design. Like other art mediums, video can be used for self-expression, narration of experience, social reportage, and as a vehicle for exploring fantastic or subjective concepts.

### Characteristics of Video.

- Immediacy: Through instant replay, recorded images and sounds may be played back immediately.
- Portability: The lightweight battery-operated Portapak (camera and recorder) offers mobility.
- Inexpensive: Aside from the original purchase of the basic equipment, video is cheaper than film. Tapes can be reused.
- Easy to operate: Video tape is fun and easy to learn. There are relatively few controls.
- Synaesthetic: Video has automatic synchronization of image and sound.
- Time-oriented. Video images are recorded within a time sequence, which makes video an excellent narrative medium.
- Long recording time: Compared to film, video has a relatively long recording time. The Portapak has 30 minutes of continuous recording time; half-inch table decks record for an hour.

### Basic Equipment.

- Video camera
- Tape deck
- Monitor
- Tape

### Additional Equipment

- Microphone and earphones
- Tripod
- Special lights if natural light is not sufficent: incandescent, quartz, or fluorescent lights.
- Editor, Mixer: Editing involves copying segments of one or more tapes onto a final edited tape. This is done electronically with an editing deck. Mixers are used for superimposing or synthesizing images from different sources onto one tape. This equipment is usually available in video labs.

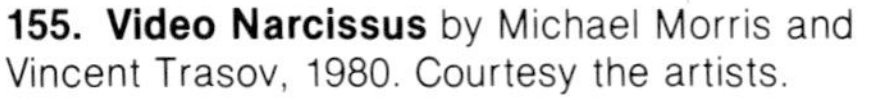

155. **Video Narcissus** by Michael Morris and Vincent Trasov, 1980. Courtesy the artists.

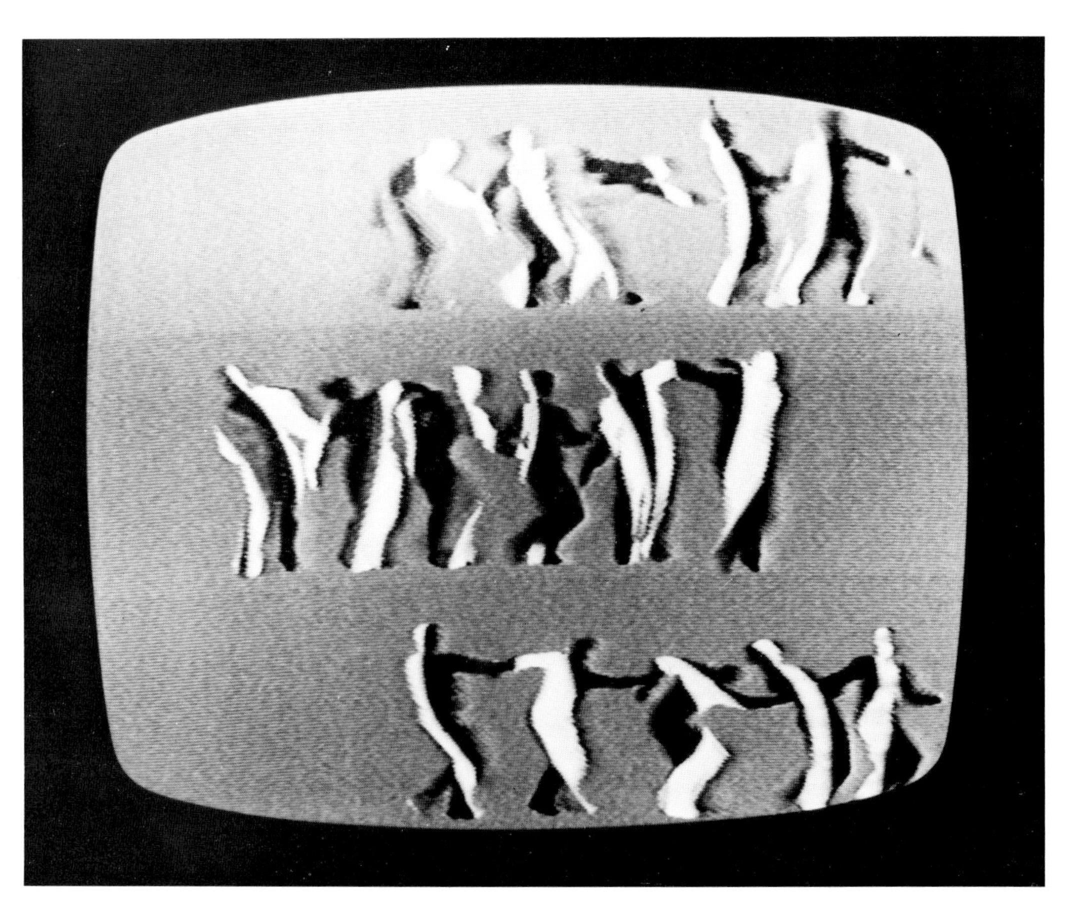

**156. Limbo: an Electronic Event for Television** by Alwin Nikolais.
Courtesy the artist.

**Differences Between Film and Video.** Motion-picture film creates the illusion of movement through the presentation of 24 still pictures per second. In video, however, no sequential images are seen on the tape. Instead, electronic impulses are stored on the tape, and are subsequently scanned electronically and translated into light and dark patterns on the TV screen. The images are in fact generated by a single dot of light, which travels at great speed across the surface of the TV tube.

## Uses for Video.

- Performance: improvisation, games, role playing, dramatizations, mime, choreographed movement, modeling wearable art, event and performance, conceptual art.
- Interview: people waiting for busses, coming out of movie houses, waiting in lines, at special events; friends, colleagues, special personalities, characters, and so on.
- Documentation: street and environmental motifs such as architecture, store facades, signs, advertising, litter, automobiles, environmental spaces; news programs with a new twist: interviewing historical or art personalities; staged events at the gym, swimming pool, park, track; competitions, games, events.
- Video Abstractions, Feedback: by pointing the camera at its own monitor, abstract patterns are generated. The particular alignment or angle of camera to monitor determines the designs: upright alignment of camera to monitor produces spiral patterns, tilted camera produces circular patterns, 90° angle produces rectangular patterns, and so on. Other special effects are created by shooting through lenticular glass, plastic lenses, or V mirrors taped to the lens.

**157. Death of an Era** by Dustin Shuler, performance event at California State University, Domingues Hills, October 23, 1980. In destroying the heaviest, longest, widest production car ever made, the artist symbolically portrayed the end of the American belief that "bigger is better." Performed before an audience of one thousand spectators, a twenty-foot common nail, nicknamed Two Ton, was dropped with the aid of a twenty-ton crane from a height of one hundred feet through the roof of a white 1959 Cadillac perched symbolically atop four oil drums. Impaled, the Caddie was then turned over on its side and left for public view for four weeks. Said Shuler of the event, "It was a good hunt, I got my limit."

**right: 158. Erak Erak! They Eat Peanuts** by Susan Nininger, 1976, clay and fiber. Courtesy the artist. Photo: Laurie Bruce.

# 5

## ACTIVITIES

### 5-1 / Wearable Art

**Concept:** Turning the human body into an art form.

**Do:** 1. Design and make an art form that can be worn on some part of the body.

2. Plan and present a fashion show.

3. Synectic costume party: dress with outrageous combinations of clothing, artifacts, makeup, and accessories.

### 5-2 / Performance Event

**Concept:** Creating an interdisciplinary, mixed-media art event.

**Do:** 1. Plan a performance event that requires people plus one of the following:

| | |
|---|---|
| Long ribbons | Newspapers |
| Bicycles | Drinking glasses and straws |
| Painted sticks | Roller skates |
| Sheets of sheer fabric | Frisbees |
| Inner tubes | Balloons |

2. Stage the event.

3. Document with 35mm photography or video.

### 5-3 / Art Fetish

**Concept:** Creating a ritual object.

**Do:** 1. Create a papier-mâché mask that is calculated to perform an imaginary magical function: a mask with the inherent power to make it snow, bring about straight "A" grades, repel the "chocolate-bar devil," or realize your most outlandish fantasy.

2. Make the mask from papier-mâché and decorate with tempera, acrylic, and/or materials such as yarn, beads, mirrors, mosaic, et cetera.

3. Plan a performance event or fashion show using the masks.

**159. Gypsy Pilot Tea Set** by Susan Nininger, 1977, clay and fiber. Courtesy the artist. Photo: Jo David.

Artist's statement: "I keep my eyes and mind open for images and ideas which in some way are fascinating, strange, or amusing, and then try to relate them to my concepts regarding costume. My idea of costume is an object, or a set of objects, which relate in some intimate way to the human body. I have tried to explore this aspect by stretching the definitions of what the human body can actually accommodate: by making costumes which have parts made of clay, wood, papier-mâché, mirror, et cetera, and also by means of creating costumes which use the body as a foundation upon which to display sculptural form. It is important to me that my costumes evoke a will to fantasize in those who view them."

## 5-4 / Imaginarium — An Environmental Bubble

**Concept:** Creating an inflatable media bubble.

**Do:** 1. Obtain materials to build a polyethylene air-supported bubble: (a) three 9' x 12' (2.7 x 3.6 m) sheets of polyethylene plastic (4 mil heavy-duty plastic) or painters' plastic drop cloths; (b) freezer tape or duct tape for joining the sections together; (c) fan for producing air and sustaining the structure in an upright state.

2. Lay out two of the polyethylene drop cloths on top of each other.

3. Tape three sides together (two long sides plus one end).

4. Take the third sheet of polyethylene — cut to 9' x 6' (2.7 x 1.8 m) in size — and tape it together to form a long tube, running freezer tape down its length.

5. Attach one end of the tube to the center of the open end of the larger form, using freezer tape to form a seal.

6. Attach the other end of the tube to the front of a household fan.

7. Inflate.

8. Cut a 4' (1.2 m) vertical slit in the bubble to act as a door. Attach a small piece of polyethylene inside of it to act as an air lock. Tape the top.

9. Use the plastic bubble as a rear-projection screen: by projecting 35mm slides or motion-picture films on it, it can serve as a "media bubble."

## 5-5 / Event Structures

**Concept:** Making structures for use in performance events.

**Do:** 1. Select one of the themes listed below.

2. Make an appropriate structure.

3. Plan a performance using the structure.

4. Present to an audience or video-tape the event.

(a) **Headbox.** Make a cardboard box with a hole in the bottom big enough for your head to fit through. Add designs, collage elements, objects, and so on to the surface (or interior, if a portion of the box is left open). Create a solo dialogue or collaborate with another "headbox" to present a three-minute performance.

(b) **Wearable Art.** Create a form inspired by the design of a sea creature, which can be worn by more than one person. Write a scenario. Video-tape a performance.

(c) **Launched Art.** Make a structure that can be launched into the air, water, or placed into a selected environment — a sandy beach, in a tree, hallway, street, et cetera.

## 5-6 / Nature Maze

**Concept:** Creating an event-structure. (an art structure used in conjunction with a performance event)

**Do:** 1. Plan an outdoor labyrinth. Select a special outdoor setting and use elements of nature as the principal components of the structure: sand, water, leaves, grass, snow, earth, trees, rocks, along with other materials such as rope, hay, cardboard, ribbon, colored sand, whiting, and so on.

2. With a small group, decide how best to construct the labyrinth. Will it involve digging, roping off areas? Create ground rules for staging a movement-event through the structure.

3. Construct the maze and stage the event.

4. Video-tape the event.

**160. Elastic Spots: a Performance Piece** by Evelyn Roth Moving Sculpture Co. Courtesy the artist.

**161. Piazza of San Cardo** by students of Rafaelo Dvorak's design class, University of California, Berkeley. The assignment: "Create a structure that somehow relates to the sun, and can also serve as a chair. Use cardboard, tape, and paint to realize the form." When linked together, the sections look very much like a small European village.

## 5-7 / Miniature City

**Concept:** Creating an architectural environment.

**Do:** 1. Create a structure that can support your own weight and can be interlocked with other similar modular structures. Use cardboard, masking tape, and acrylic or latex paint.

2. As a class project, assemble all of the units to form an architectural cluster.



**right: 162.** Although it appears to be a pipe, it is also the subject for transformation by the fertile imagination.

## 5-8 / Improvisation

**Concept:** Acting out a concept.

Improvisation is an "acting out" type of creative activity that involves specific problem-stating, problem-solving situations. Scenarios are not planned in advance but evolve spontaneously during performances.

**Do:** Select and participate in one of the following activities:

**Transformation** (group activity). Seat participants in a circle. Start by having one person use an imaginary object, such as a hair dryer. He then passes it on to the next person who transforms it — turns it into a horn, for example — then passes it on to the next person in the circle until all participants have had an opportunity to act out a transformation.

**Stage Hands** (two people). In preparation for this performance, first cut out a "window" from a large sheet of cardboard. Two people seated directly behind the cardboard should be completely screened, with only their hands showing. Using the window as a stage area, create a scenario for two hands: have the hands act out a story through symbolic gestures. Use accessory props if required.

**Machine** (group activity). In this collective improvisation, one person starts the activity by acting out the movements of a part of a machine or device — the pistons of a train, for example. One by one, each of the other participants joins in, mimicking additional moving parts (wheels, cogs, cams) until the "machine" is fully functioning. The group does not have to symbolize a known machine (such as a car, truck, or train), but may portray a Rube Goldberg-type nonsense device. On the second go-round, have each person add sound effects to accompany their movements.

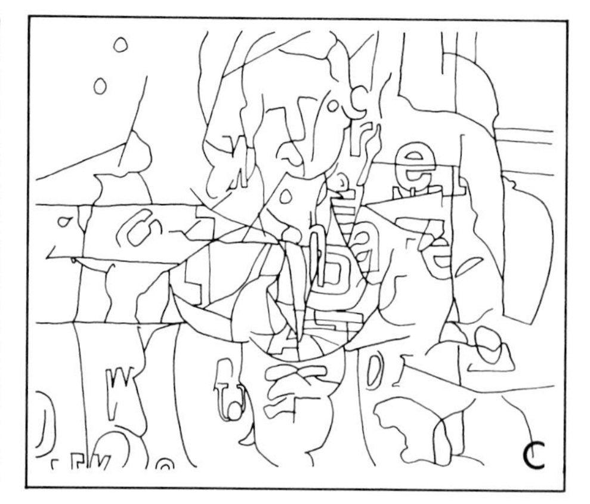


## 5-9 / TV Art Game

**Concept:** Documenting fragments of TV images. (Courtesy Tom Ockerse.)

There lingers on the mental screen an amalgamated labyrinth of superimposed images from any given TV program. Who knows what psychological impressions are generated from the countless verbal-visual signals, images, and symbols that form the total pastiche etched in our mind's eye. This art game, to some extent, provokes curious afterthoughts regarding the implications of such stratified images.

**Do:** 1. Tape a sheet of translucent drafting paper to a TV screen.

2. Establish the ground rules for making image tracings. For example:

(a) Trace curved lines from TV images within a 30-minute period, switching channels every three minutes.

(b) Trace only straight lines from a 30-minute program.

(c) Make up your own ground rules for creating additional tracings.

## 5-10 / Synectic Design Game

**Concept:** Creating designs by mixing dissimilar images.

**Do:** 1. Divide a 12" x 18" (30 x 45 cm) sheet of white drawing paper into a grid of 24 3" squares.

2. Draw shapes along the top and left side of the gridded paper.

3. Fill in the remaining squares with additional shapes that are amalgamations of the original drawings. (vertical-horizontal intersections)

**above : 163. TV Documentracings** by Tom Ockerse, felt tip pen on tracing paper. Courtesy the artist. (a) Only straight lines were traced from various programs within a thirty minute period, (b) only curved lines traced within a thirty minute program, (c) combined straight and curved lines traced from a thirty minute program.

**below: 164. Synectic Design** Game by Joseph Cranston, pen and ink. Courtesy the artist.

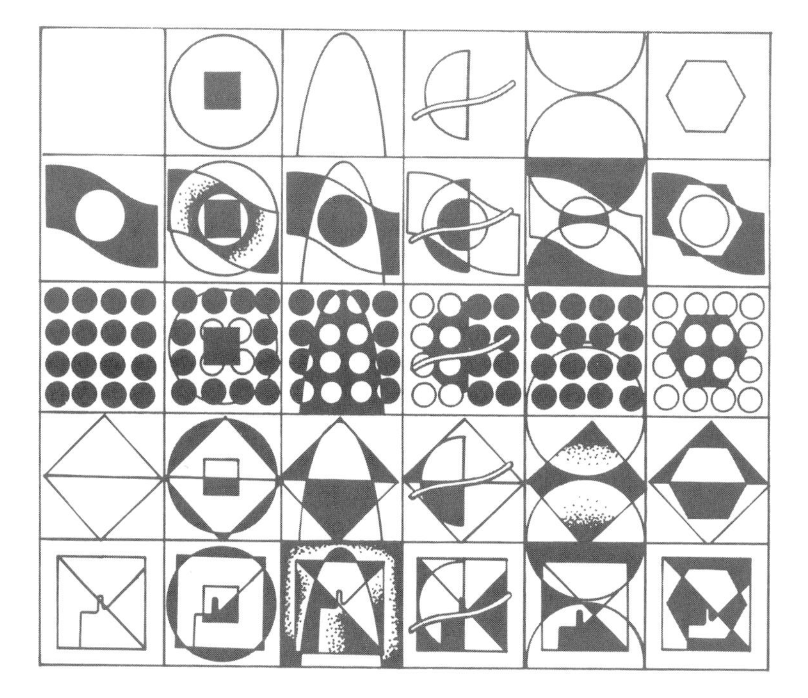

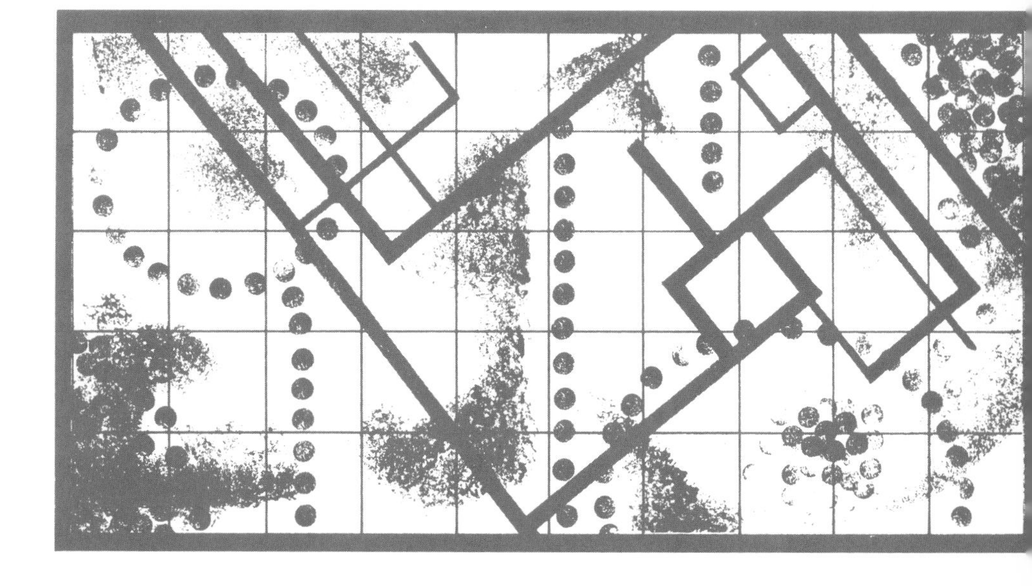

**right: 165. Galactica.** An art game by Nicholas Roukes.

## 5-11 / Galactica

**Concept:** Playing an art-based game.

*Galactica* is a mural-making game that requires six players.

**Scenario:** Three different types of creatures live in *Galactica:* the *Linezos, Amorphs,* and *Zots.* In order to communicate with other forms of intelligent life in the universe, all three participate in the creation of a *Zenograph,* a mural that incorporates three different styles of graphic expression.

**Styles of Expression:** Linezos express themselves by making only line designs or shapes that result from the use of lines. Amorphs express themselves by making only amorphous nebulous shapes, or shapes with round or soft edges. Zots express themselves by making only dots and dot patterns. (Only abstract patterns are used in the designs; Galactic creatures do not use representational images.)

**Playing the Game:** Pair up each group of six people so there are two Linezos, two Amorphs, and two Zots. Have as many groups as there are class members; each group will create their own mural.

**Score-Plans:** Each team makes a Score-Plan, a preliminary design created within the constraints of each group's mode of graphic expression. A score-plan is made on a 5" x 10" (12.5 x 25.4 cm) rectangle divided into 1" grids, producing a grid pattern of 50 1" squares.

**Score-Plan Tools:** Each group uses special tools to create their score-plans: Linezos use only felt pens; Amorphs use only small sponges, 1" (2.54 cm) square; Zots use only pencil erasers and rubber-stamp pads. (All use acrylic or tempera paint to create designs.)

15 minutes is allocated for the creation of the score-plans. Score-plan designs may cover only up to 50% of the surface area of the 5" x 10" rectangle.

**Action: Object of the Game.** Each team, armed with a score-plan, seeks to transfer the complete details of their design (square by square) to a large sheet of gridded butcher paper: Tape a 35" x 70" (89 x 178 cm) sheet of buff or colored butcher or display paper to the wall. Use white chalk to make horizontal and vertical lines spaced 7" (17.8 cm) apart, producing a grid pattern of 50 7" squares.

**Limitations:** Each group can work only when it hears its own music. Create in advance a tape cassette of three different types of recorded music interspersed in three- to five-minute segments. As each group hears its music, it goes to work on the mural while the previous group retires.

**Mural Tools:** In producing the mural or Zenograph, each team uses large-scale versions of the tools used to make the preliminary score-plans. Linezos use 1/2" or 4" (1.3 or 10.2 cm) paint rollers with acrylic or tempera paint. Amorphs use 4" x 6" (10.2 x 15.2 cm) sponges and acrylic or tempera paint. Zots use tools made of 1" (2.5 cm) diameter sponges attached to the ends of dowels, with acrylic or tempera paint. (Have separate rollers, sponges, and printing sticks on hand for each color to be used.) The tape cassette is played repeatedly until the mural is completed to the mutual satisfaction of the three groups.

**Further Activity:** Invent your own art-based game.

**right: 166.** The process of cutting and shifting images can be carried out according to prescribed "game rules" or through chance methods.

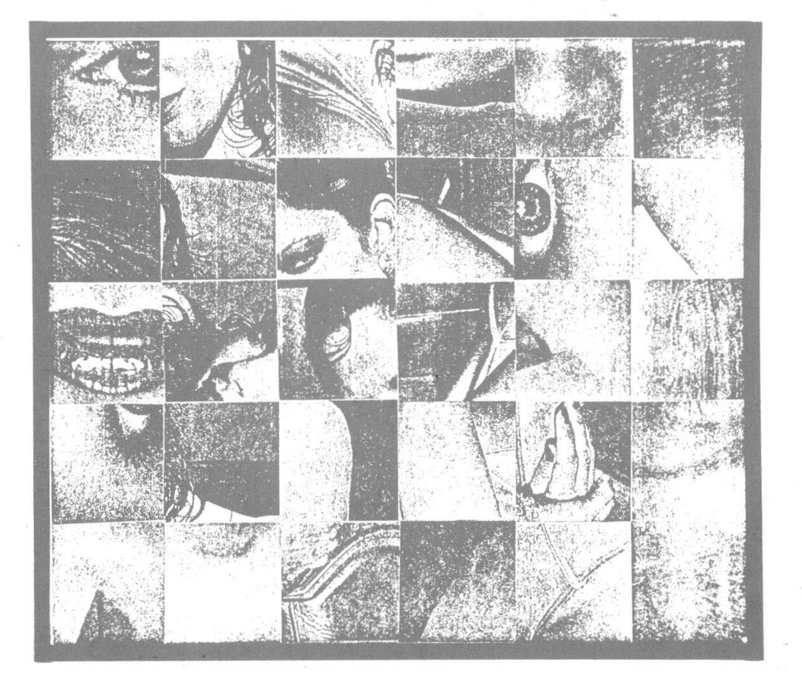

## 5-12 / Reassembled Components

**Concept:** Altering images by shifting grid components.

**Do:** 1. Find a large photographic image and divide it into 1" (2.5 cm) squares.

2. Cut the image into squares and reassemble it on a sheet of black construction paper.

3. Shift the components to create an entirely different design pattern.

## 5-13 / Sound Sculpture

**Concept:** Creating a three-dimensional sculpture that produces sound effects.

**Do:** 1. Collect materials and objects that produce different sounds.

2. Construct a three-dimensional sculpture with them. The structure may involve spectator participation, insofar as it can be "played" like a musical instrument; react to environmental conditions on its own (having elements that capture wind, rain, et cetera) and translate them into sounds through appropriate devices; or be a kinetic sculpture programmed with switches, timers, or other devices.

**above: 167. Sound Sculpture** by Donald Finberg, 1978, mixed media. Courtesy the artist. This construction is designed to appeal to both audio as well as visual perception.

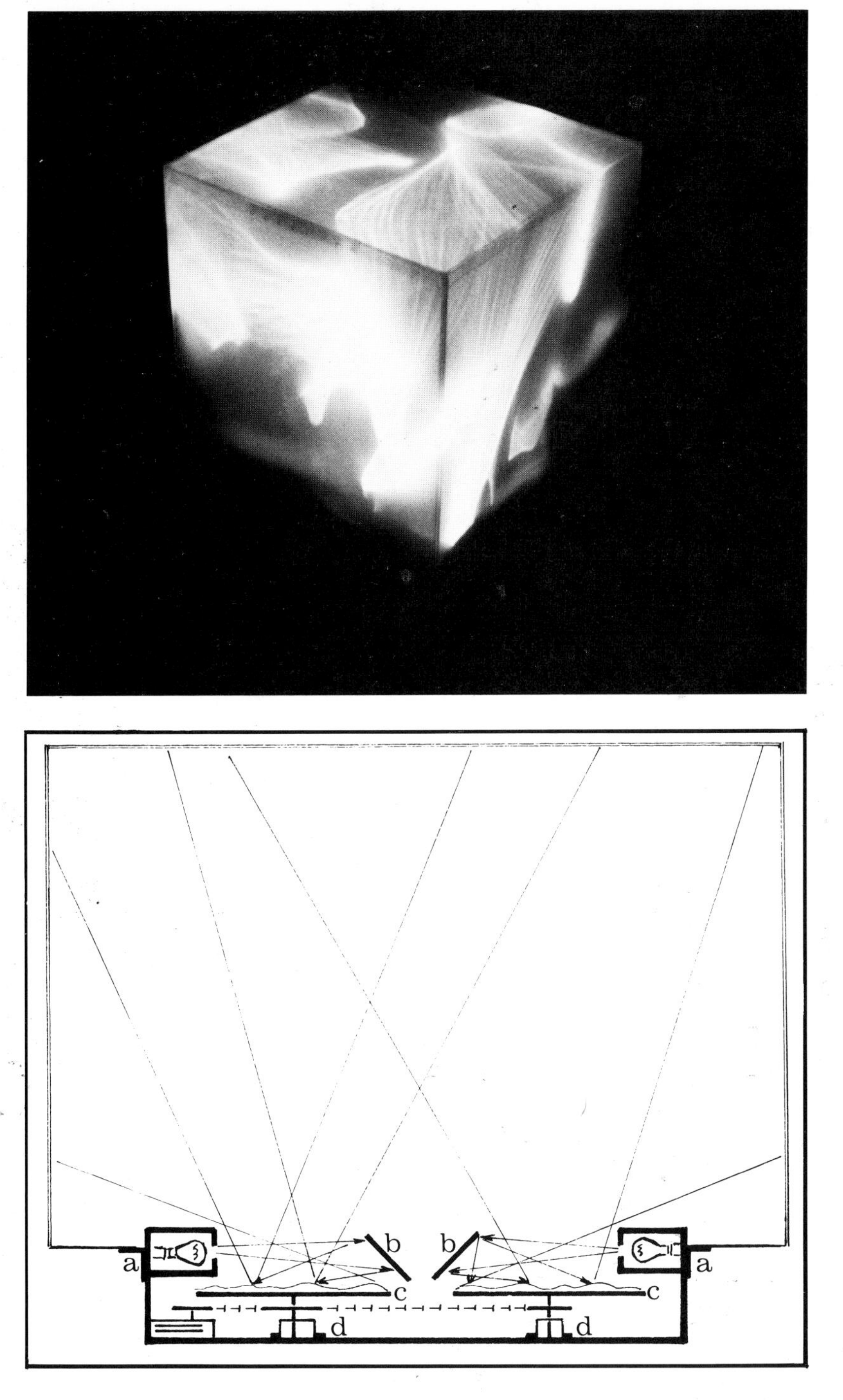


**top: 168. Kinoptic Light Sculpture** by Valerios Caloutsis, 1971, 19-1/2" x 19-1/2" x 19-1/2" (49.5 x 49.5 x 49.5 cm), acrylic over kinetic element. A transluscent plastic box is placed over the kinoptic system (shown in the diagram), which creates an on-going program of moving light images. The variation and complexity of the program is determined by the configuration of the mirrors on the revolving turntable, and the speed of the motor, which determines the length of the program cycle.

**above: 169. Diagram of the kinoptic light system:** (a) Light source: a 40 watt clear filament bulb, (b) fixed mirror, (c) turntable with mirrorized plastic shapes, (d) 1 r.p.m. motor.

**above: 170. Inflatos** by Malcolm Gimse. Courtesy the artist. 1mm polyethylene was used to create this event-structure. Various sections were taped together with freezer tape to make air-tight volumes; a plastic "umbilical cord" led to a 19" fan, which kept the forms inflated.

**right: 171. Labyrinth** by Robert Morris. 1974, Masonite, plywood. Installed at the Institute of Contemporary Art, Philadelphia. Photo: Will Brown.

# CHAPTER 6

# PARADOX

*One of the distinguishing characteristics of the true work of art is that it is able to both contain and express different meanings – meanings which may in fact contradict one another. A fruitful ambiguity is in fact one of the great strengths of the art of the past decade.*

Edward Lucie-Smith

The word *paradox* means "beyond credibility." It can also be used to denote an image, statement, or proposition that seems to contradict logic, but when further investigated may appear to be well-founded.

## Visual Paradox

Visual paradoxes are graphic images that present incompatible information to the brain. M.C. Escher's drawings, for example, seem to say that "nothing is as it appears — there are *other* laws of logic that draw the universe and all of its elements together."

René Magritte's images play a successful cat-and-mouse game with the viewer's perceptions as well. In his strange paintings, laws of gravity and natural evolution are brazenly defied; his works have been described as "visual booby traps," triggered by the viewer's futile attempts to rationally comprehend the significance of the strange image combinations presented. Yet, because we have such an innate fascination for puzzles, Magritte's work is strongly compelling and his images remain suspended in our mind's eye. We in fact enjoy the cat-and-mouse game that the artist plays with us. John Graham struck a vital chord when he wrote that the origin of art lies in the human longing for enigma. Through the contemplation of the eccentric imagery of such artists as Escher and Magritte, we as viewers are asked to reevaluate our own definition of "reality."

**below: 172. Slave Market with the Disappearing Bust of Voltaire** by Salvador Dali, 1940, 18-1/2" x 25-3/4" (46.3 x 65.5 cm), oil on canvas. Courtesy Salvador Dali Museum, Cleveland, Ohio. Collection Mr. and Mrs. A. Reynolds Morse. Here is a clever optical illusion: The bust of Voltaire is cryptically implanted within the landscape. As in optical illusion figures, the images mysteriously "flip-flop" upon contemplation, revealing the latent image.

**173. Delusions of Grandeur** by René Magritte, 1948, 39'' x 32'' (99 x 81 cm), oil on canvas. Courtesy Hirshorn Museum, Washington, D.C.

**174. Zoo Keepers** by Sandra Jackman, 1980, 9'' x 7'' x 10-3/4'' (22.8 x 17.8 x 27.3 cm), assemblage. Courtesy the artist.

# Surrealistic Perceptions

The word *surreal* has been attributed to Guillaume Apollinaire who first used it in 1917 in his play, *Les Mamelles des Tirésias.* He used the term to describe man's ability to create objects and images not found in nature. He cited the wheel as an example of an object that could never be produced by nature, and therefore existing *beyond* nature — in the realm of the "surreal."

From such examples, Apollinaire concluded that science far excelled the arts in its ability to produce surreal inventions. By his original definition, science today would still outstrip the arts in this distinction. The cornucopia of contemporary "surreal" inventions — nuclear reactors, machine intelligence, advances in medicine, space vehicles, ICBMs, and DNA recombinants — are indeed mind-boggling.

Freud's discovery of the *unconscious,* however, added a new dimension to Apollinaire's definition. The bizarre objects of science now took second place to the "mental objects" springing forth from the subconscious mind. And André Breton, who wrote *The Surrealistic Manifesto* in the early 1900s, defined surrealism as "pure psychic automatism." Breton saw it as a means of exploring the fantastic world of the subconscious mind, and stated in his manifesto: "I believe in the transmutation of two seemingly contradictory states, dream and reality, into a sort of absolute reality — of *surreality.*"

**below: 177. Souvenir** by Tetsumi Kudo, 1965, 47-1/4" x 26-1/2" (120 x 67 cm), mixed media. Courtesy the artist. A birdcage is transformed into an outrageous image; recognizable fragments of human anatomy are imprisoned within the bizarre environment.

**below: 175. Duality** by Juan Manuel De La Rosa, 1979 pen-and-ink drawing. Courtesy Mexican Museum, San Francisco. Photo: Blair Partridge.

**right: 176. Portrait** by Vincente Ameztoy, 1970, 55" x 45" (140 x 114 cm). Courtesy Galeria Juana Mordo, Madrid.

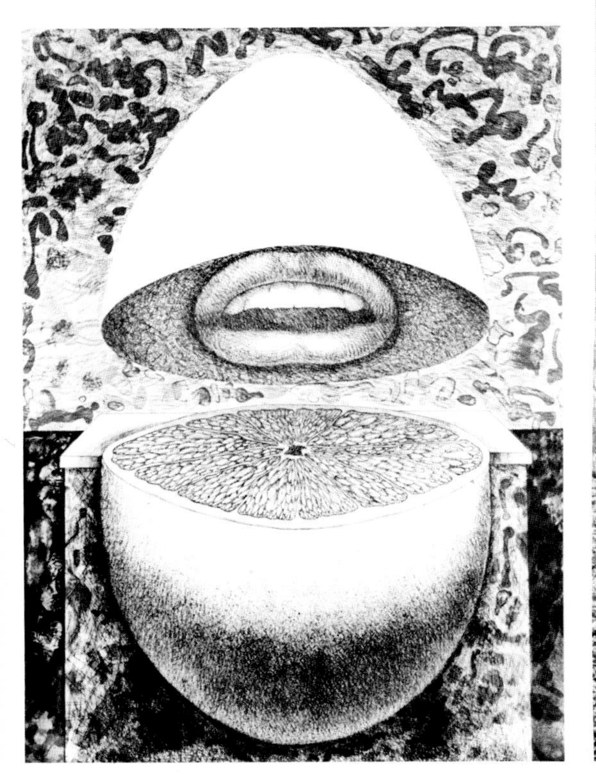

Surrealism can be described in two ways: (1) It is an ideology or school of thought organized in the early 1920s in Paris; André Breton was the titular head of this group composed of artists and writers. (2) More broadly, surrealism can be thought of as a particular kind of perception or vision that expresses itself through fantasy, dreams, and the irrational.

Because fantastic thought originates through both logical and illogical mental processes, Breton's definition of surrealism (''pure psychic automatism'') was felt to be too restricting by many succeeding artists. Consequently, the definition was later extended by Marcel Duchamp to include ''conscious thought acting upon the materials discovered by the unconscious.'' ''Ready-made'' objects were subsequently altered by conscious deliberation to suit the subjective desires of the artist.

**178. Divisibilité Indefinie** by Yves Tanguy, 1942, 40'' x 35'' (101.6 x 88.9 cm), oil on canvas. Courtesy Albright-Knox Art Gallery, Buffalo, New York.

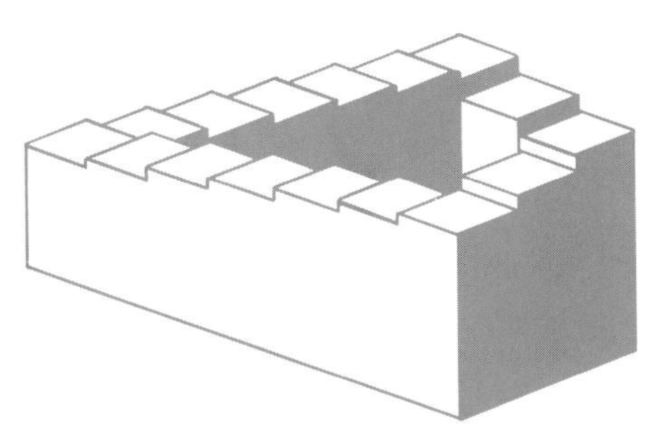

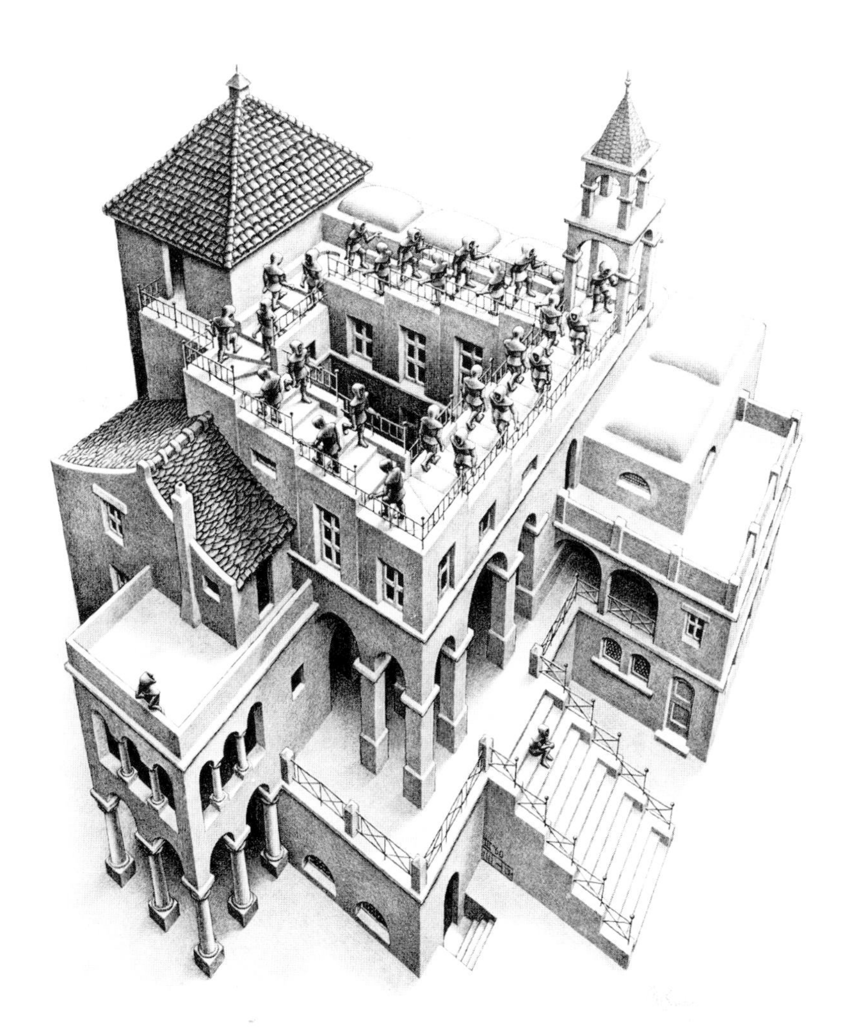

**above:179. Optical Illusion.** This basic "flip-flop" design is incorporated within M.C. Escher's composition *Ascending Descending* (right).

**right: 180. Ascending and Descending** by M.C. Escher, 1960, 13-3/4"x 11-1/4" (350 x 285 cm), lithograph. Courtesy Gemeentemuseum, The Hague. A remarkable optical illusion is produced in this drawing through the implantation of an illogical optical figure.
The monks shown in the composition appear to be fighting a hopeless battle in climbing the endless staircase.

**lower right: 181. Death and the Bourgeois** by Mathaus Merian the Elder, 18th century, engraving. In this "flip-flop" figure, the optical illusion is realized only when the image is reversed.

**Optical Illusions.** Optical illusions are also visual paradoxes. They are *misleading images,* insofar as they cause us to perceive things somewhat differently from what is actually presented. Optical illusions trick the eyes and cause them to send unreliable information to the brain. These quirks are induced by the peculiarities of visual perception, which are inherent in the physiological limitations of the eyes and the characterstics of binocular vision.

A study of the dynamics of visual perception can be of great help to the artist concerned with Op Art and other illusionary effects. Two authoritative books on the subject are *Eye and Brain* and *The Intelligent Eye,* both by R.L. Gregory.

In optical art (or Op Art), the artist systematically probes into the realms of motion, space, and optics and the laws of human perception.

Examine some of the optical illusions in this chapter and see how they are used as a basis for creating optical paintings by such artists as Victor Vasarely, Bridget Riley, Carlos Cruz-Diez, Francois Morrellet, Reginald Neal, Larry Poons, Gerald Oster, Julio LeParc, Francois Yvaral, and Richard Anuszkeiwicz.

**Latent Images.** Latent images are images that are concealed or camouflaged within an art form. *The Disappearing Bust of Voltaire* by Dali is a good example of how an artist uses this pictorial device.

**below center: 182. Maze** by Joe Tilson, 1979, wood. Courtesy the artist.

**below left: 183. Les Religieuses** by James Douglass, 1975, 10" x 12-3/4" x 3-1/2" (25.4 x 32.4 x 8.9 cm), wood, paper, ceramic. Courtesy the artist.

**below right: 184. Untitled** by Joseph Cornell, 1956-58, 10" x 15" (25.4 x 38 cm), mixed media. Courtesy John Berggruen Gallery, San Francisco. Photo: Eric Pollitzer. Cornell's "little worlds in boxes" are inspired by a personal vision. Refusing to arrange visual elements into mere juxtapositions of universally understood symbols, the artist protects the magic of illusion and ambiguity, and allows the viewer to project his own fantasy into the work.

# Labyrinths

Labyrinths are intricate deceptive structures designed in one of two ways: in the first type, the participant is offered a guided pathway from point "A" to point "Z"; the second type is a complex structure of dead ends and blind passages, an environment in which one can easily become confused or lost. (Symbolically, the unconscious mind has been compared to a labyrinth, since both have inaccessible corridors and compartments.)

The labyrinth was often integrated into the architectural design of medieval churches. Such a labyrinth usually formed part of the nave and consisted of variously colored tiles or stone slabs, arranged in a square, circular, or octagonal pattern. Because they were considered symbolic of the path taken by Christ from Jerusalem to Calvary, they were followed by the pious offering prayers in church ceremonies. Some labyrinths of this type have survived, such as that of Chartres Cathedral in France.

Robert Morris's wooden *Labyrinth,* constructed at the Institute of Contemporary Art at the University of Pennsylvania in Philadelphia, is a modern example of an artist utilizing the labyrinth as an art form. In 1970, Dennis Oppenheim used bales of hay to create a maze in a cowfield of 20,000 square feet. Cows were found to "obey the rules of the maze," finding their way in one end to discover food at the other.

**Fantasy Boxes.** Many of the early surrealists collected interesting junk from secondhand stores and flea markets. They were on the constant lookout for objects that, when seen among a large number of other articles, somehow seemed to possess a strange fascination or special charm. It was not mere trash that they sought, but special objects that mysteriously provided surprise solutions to their art forms when incorporated with other objects. The box format seems to have originated with Breton and Max Ernst, and continues to be a favorite format for contemporary artists concerned with the portrayal of subjective imagery: Fernandez Arman, Jean Crotti, Tetsumi Kudo, Lucas Samaras, H.C. Westerman, Robert Rauschenberg, Alphonse Ossorio, Louise Nevelson, George Brecht, and Joseph Cornell.

Cornell's fantasy boxes are like tiny stage sets incorporating objects such as photographs, astrological charts, glass marbles, crystal, stuffed birds, and apothecary jars stuffed with assorted articles. His boxes seem to chart a personal journey into his own special universe, which has been described by K.L. McShine as, "a universe of the marvelous, of paradox, and enigma — of questions without answers and of answers without questions."

**above left: 185. NeoDada** by Robert Whitson, 1975, 7" x 7" (17.8 x 17.8 cm), collage. Xerox print. Courtesy the artist. Mimicking the collage techniques of early dadaists, the artist carefully cuts and assembles images from steel engravings found in various catalogues. A Xerox machine is used to duplicate the collage.

**above right: 186. Lovis Corinth in Vermont,** from the series *Art in Context: Homage to Walter Benjamin,*© Manual (Edward Hill and Suzanne Bloom) mixed media. Courtesy the artists.

**Dada.** Dada, a European anti-art movement lasting from 1916 to 1922, was intended as a form of social protest by disillusioned artists of the period. These artists respected only the creeds of chance and disorder — their "works" and "performances" were absurd and ludicrous: Duchamp signed a urinal *R. Mutt* and presented it as an art form; others threw papers to canvas and glued them in place as they fell; paint-laden brushes were shot from toy cannons to create blobs on canvas; artists recited "poetry" by uttering gibberish and nonsense sounds, and so forth. Dada was not entirely a negative movement, however, as it served to inspire the evolution of Surrealism, Assemblage, stream-of-consciousness poetry, and Abstract Expressionism.

**Imagery and Chance Variations.** J. Allan Hobson, director of neurophysiology at Harvard University, writes that only through *the play of chance* can new arrangements of biological information be achieved. He contends that mutation — the chance variation of genetic information — is well established as the creative factor in the evolution of life species. Mutations occur not only within DNA's molecular structure, but also within the realm of information processing, especially in that of dreams. Hobson states that this important feature of the new theory of dreams liberates us from the prior constraints of the narrative approach, from fundamental psychic determinism. There is a large degree of chance in both dream and thought processes, he argues, that allows for the generation of entirely new images, new sequences of images, and new compositions of new sequences.

In art, as in nature, chance performs a kind of miracle. Form and design in nature are influenced by the combined effects of chance happenings and homeostasis (homeostasis being nature's special ability to re-establish equilibrium once any system has been disturbed). In the realm of art, the unconscious intelligence of the artist stemming from the right hemisphere of the brain thrives when fed chance input. However, in order to recognize the importance of chance, the artist must be intellectually and creatively prepared. As Louis Pasteur said, "Chance favors *only* the prepared mind." The left brain (the logical side) serves as the

**above: 187. A Little Shade Near Nowhere** by Robert Bourden, 1980, mixed media. Courtesy the artist.

**below: 188. Mobius Strip 11** by M.C. Escher, 1963, 17-7/8" x 8-1/8" (45.5 x 20.7 cm), wood engraving. Courtesy Gemeentemuseum, The Hague.

**below right: 189. A Splash of Reality** by Patti Warashina, 1980, 16" x 16" x 9-1/2" (40.6 x 40.6 x 24 cm), ceramic. Courtesy the artist.

"homeostat," re-establishing order whenever reason is disturbed by chance input. Paradoxically, accidents or chance interventions can be used as creative tools by the artist, if they are allowed to wrest creative control from the conscious mind, and if the unconscious mind is given free reign. Psychologists tell us that there are two ways of knowing: An *intuitive,* inside way based on instinct and subconscious perception, and a *scientific,* outside way based on observation and measurement. Psychologists often refer to intuitive knowledge as *felt knowledge,* in contrast to verbally reasoned thought. The artist who works spontaneously is guided by "feelings of correctness," without benefit of premeditated thinking. To those artists who value the importance of subjective approaches in creating art, these words from Rudyard Kipling are particularly meaningful:

> When your Daemon is in charge do not
> try to think consciously.
> Drift, wait and obey . . .
> Walk delicately, lest he should withdraw.

Discovery by chance, accident, or spontaneity is called *serendipitous.* Jean Arp, in writing on the subject, alluded to a "mysterious order" within the realm of chance happenings:

> I declare that my works, like nature, were ordered according to the laws of chance; chance being a limited part of an unfathomable raison d'être of an order that is inaccessible in its totality.

**Fantasizing.** Why do we fantasize? Why do we enjoy daydreaming? Psychologists tell us that only sane men dream. Creative people put "handlebars" on their fantasies in order to create art forms and unique structures. Only through the mobilization of fantasy do great ideas and works of art become reality.

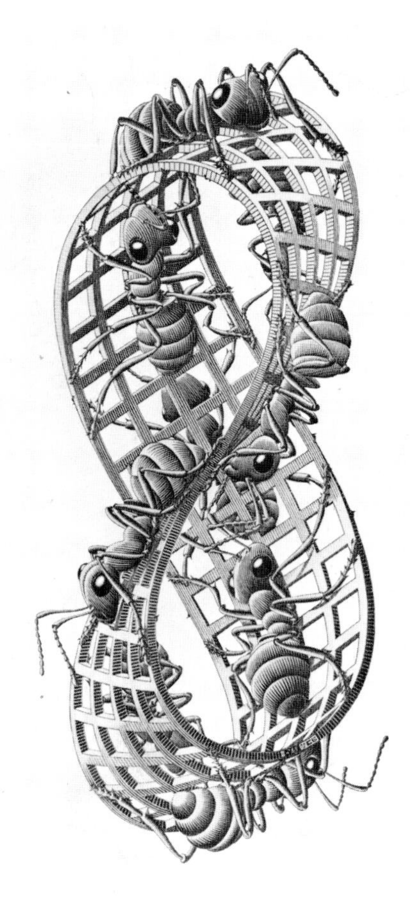

---

*Pity us, wrote Appolinaire, we who are enduring this endless quarrel between order and adventure.*
André Malraux

## Optical Illusions.

*Have you more strange illusions, yet more mists, through which the weak eye may be led to error?* Beaumont and Fletcher, *The Hungry Courtier*, 1607.

Optical illusions are visual deceptions; our eyes are fooled into presenting unreliable data to the brain. These effects are due largely to the quirks of human perception. The diagrams on this and the next page are examples of images that are violently unstable to human perception. Study them carefully. Many will suddenly "flip" to present new perceptions.

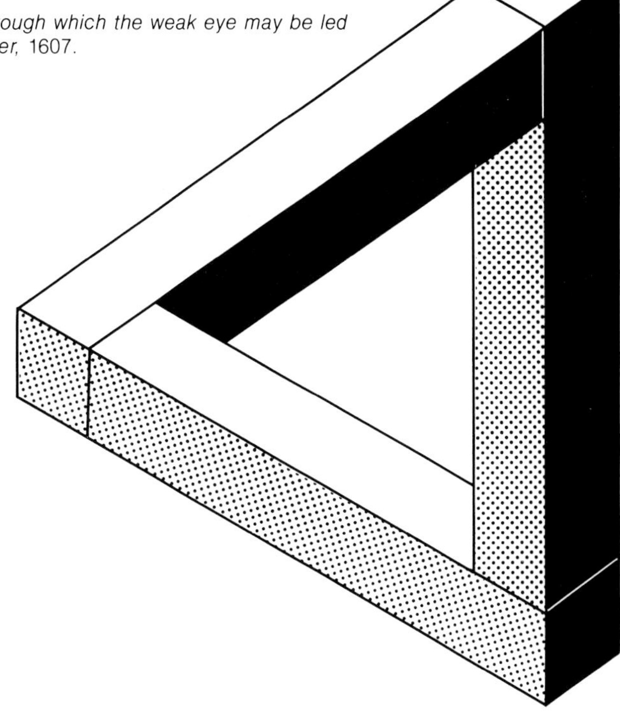

**right: 190. Impossible Structure.** The impossible triangle of L.S. and R. Penrose. The three-dimensional shape that is implied in this design cannot possibly exist in actuality.

**below: 191. Vibrating Design.** Closely spaced parallel lines generate powerful vibration fields, creating an "on-off" flicker. They also give false cues to the retinal cones, activating the perception of color. Courtesy Dover publications.

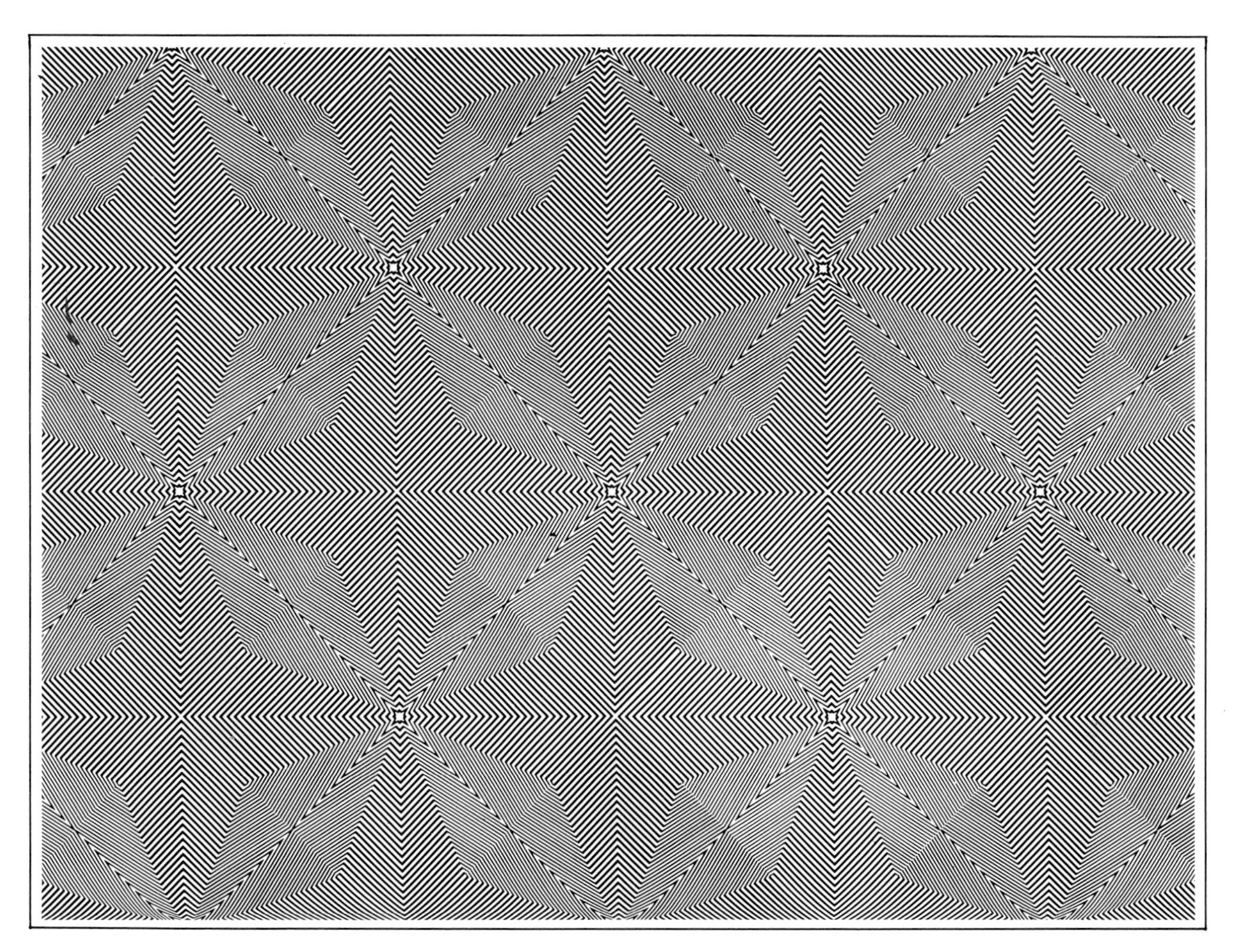

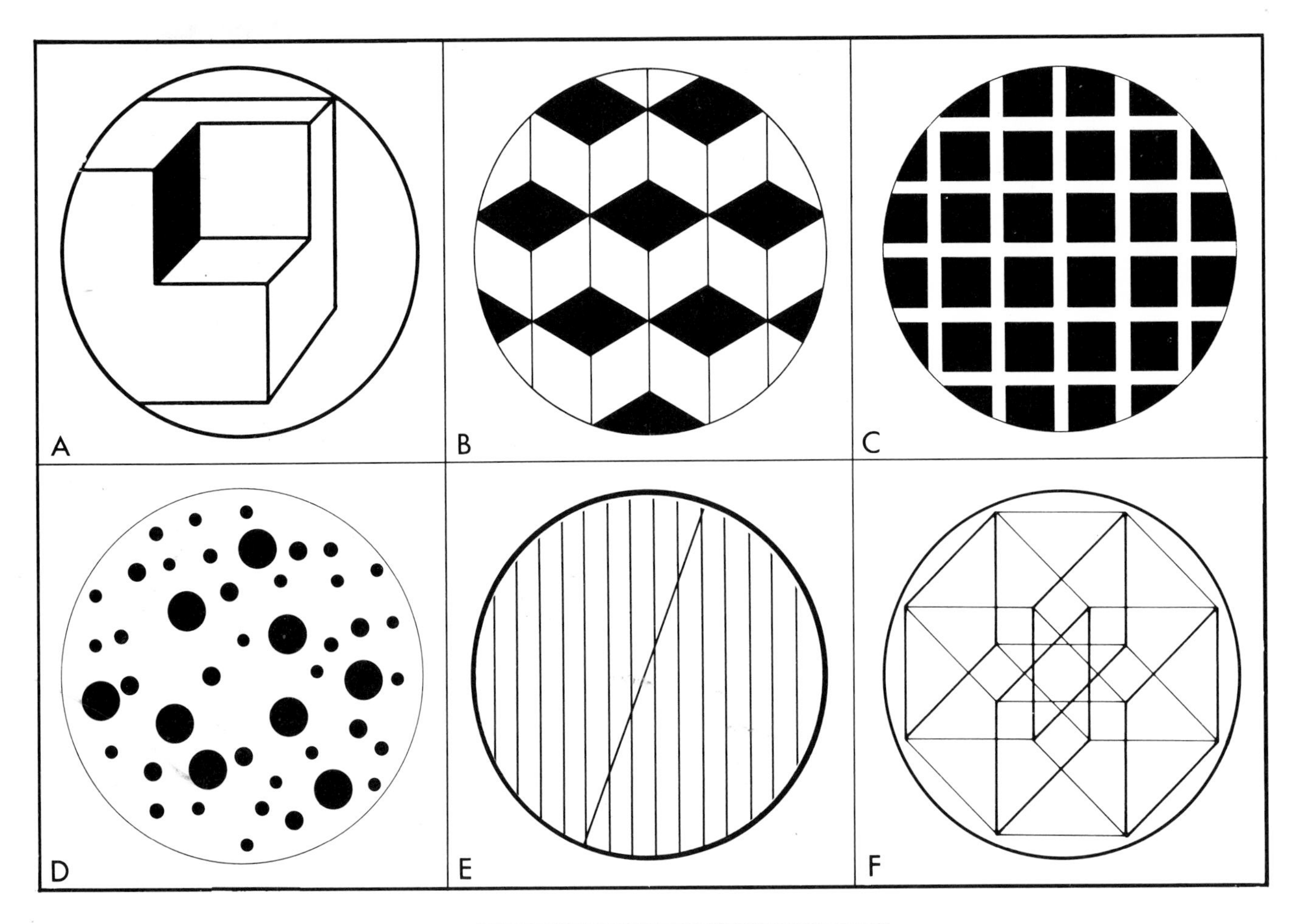


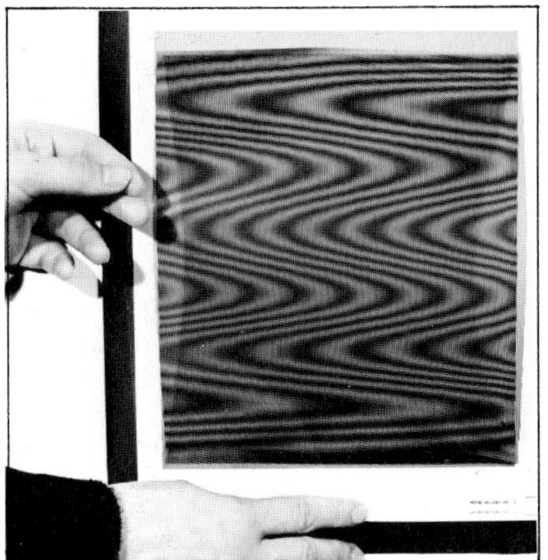

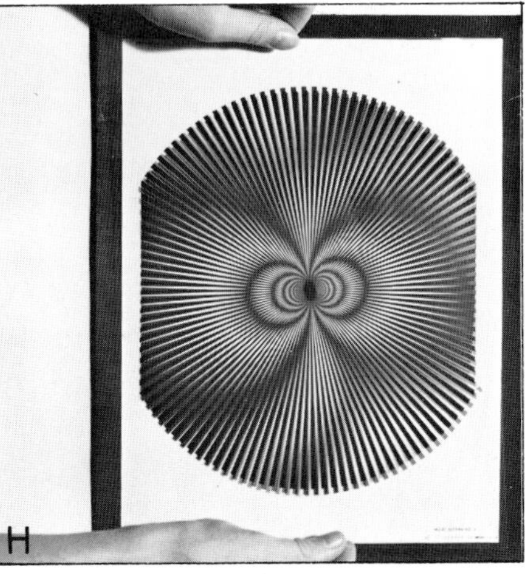


**192. Optical Illusion Figures**
A. *Positive-Negative "Flip-Flop".* Study the design carefully until it "flips" to produce opposite volumetric illusions.

B. *Triple Equivocal Figure.* The drawing may be perceived either as a flat design composed of black diamonds and parallel lines on a two-dimensional plane, or as a three-dimensional illusion of stacked cubes. Also, the cubes "flip" with the black shapes becoming either the tops or bottoms of the cubes.

C. *Illusory Shapes.* Gray shapes "pop" at the intersections of the white lines, but seem to vanish when an attempt is made to focus on them.

D. *Afterimage.* This random dot pattern demonstrates how negative afterimages interrelate with positive black dots. The combined dot patterns create a kind of "Choreography" as the eye chases the white dots. As the eye attempts to focus on the perceived white afterimages, they immediately vanish.

E. *Illusion of a Fragmenting Line.* When a single line crosses a grating of parallel lines at angles of less than 45 degrees, the line appears to break up.

F. *Multiple Volumes.* A great number of three-dimensional shapes can be made to "flip-flop"within this design.
G.H. *Moiré Patterns.* Superimposing two designs composed of parallel lines or dots printed on transparent acetate produces strong Moiré patterns. Courtesy Edmunds Scientific Company.

6

## ACTIVITIES

below center: **193. Untitled.** by James Douglass, 1977, 7-1/4" x 9" x 2" (18.4 x 22.9 x 5 cm), mixed media. Courtesy the artist.

**bottom: 194. Ann Sheridan Legend** by Sahato Fiorello, 1975, 18" x 12" x 6" (45.7 x 30.5 x 15.2 cm), mixed media. Courtesy Orlando Gallery, Encino, California.

**right: 195. Totem** by Dan Lopez, 1980, mixed media. Courtesy the artist.

### 6-1 / Surreal Totem

**Concept:** Making a subjective sculpture from "ready-mades."

**Do:** 1. Obtain 20 clear plastic drinking glasses.

2. Collect and arrange various objects and selected articles within the glasses: photographic images, designs, industrial gadgets and electronic parts, miniature toys, dolls, clock parts, charts, et cetera. Manipulate or transform the objects prior to assembly. The interior spaces of the glasses may also be altered, using paint, melted wax, candle smoke, excelsior, colored plaster, packing material. Make some interior spaces visibly clear, others obscure.

3. Glue the glasses rim to rim to form a totem.

4. Mount vertically on a base, add a nameplate and title.

### 6-2 / Unnatural Landscapes

**Concept:** Creating surrealistic landscapes in a box.

**Do:** Integrate two- or three-dimensional mediums such as photo images, found objects, carved, modeled, or painted forms, within the space of a small box or boxlike receptacle.

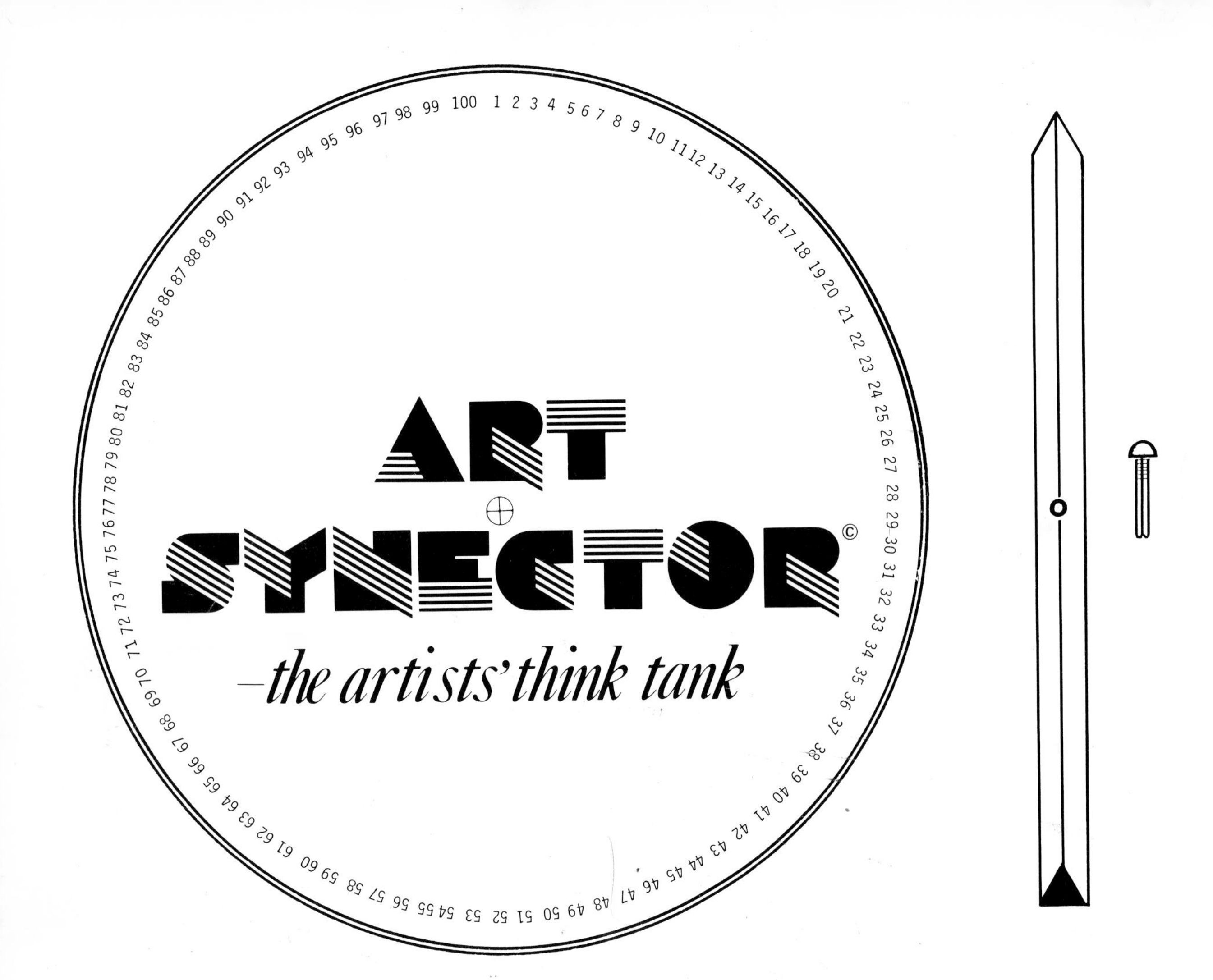


196. The Art Synector provides a serendipitous way to prod the imagination and generate art problems.

## 6-3 / The Art Synector

Photocopy this page and assemble the Art Synector on illustration board.

**Concept:** Evolving cohesive structures and art forms from disparities. The Art Synector is a think tank calculated to prod the imagination by presenting highly disparate elements for conciliation. Here's how it works: (1) Spin the arrow three times. (2) Find the corresponding words to the numbers on the accompanying chart. Fill in the words to complete the "Synectic art problem." (3) Reconcile the seemingly contradictory sentence in any way you desire. There are no "wrong" answers. Allow ideas — however outlandish — to fly freely. Eventually, cohesive ideas will emerge from the seemingly chaotic problem. Remember, there is virtually nothing that cannot be connected to something else in a physical, intellectual, or psychological sense.

**Do:** 1. Select an art problem from the Art Synector following the directions above.

2. Write out ideas and "proposals" on paper.

3. Select one of the ideas and visualize it in a medium of your choice — a painting, design, sculpture, mixed-media art form, video-tape, or performance piece.

---

*Creativity is that marvellous capacity to grasp mutually distinct realities and draw a spark from their juxtaposition.*
Max Ernst

**The Synectic Art Problem:**
**CREATE AN ART FORM THAT INVOLVES________, ________, AND ________.**

1. Boxes
2. Alteration
3. Anti-gravity
4. Love
5. Light
6. Violence
7. Constellations
8. Dream
9. Fluids
10. Alienation
11. Imprisonment
12. Grid Structure
13. Freedom
14. Astrology
15. Identity
16. Chance
17. Portrait
18. Hostility
19. Mutation
20. Growth
21. Conflict
22. Conformity
23. Wood
24. Compression
25. Linking
26. Labels
27. Ritual
28. Pleasure
29. Illusion
30. Symmetry
31. Tubes
32. War
33. Window
34. Violation
35. Theft
36. Calligraphy
37. Fingers
38. Junk
39. Insignia
40. Jail
41. Jars
42. Headlines
43. Wheels
44. Wings
45. Science Fiction
46. Trap
47. Scissors
48. Transparency
49. Puzzle
50. Utopia
51. Mythology
52. Microstructure
53. Serialization
54. Automobiles
55. Cityscape
56. Birds
57. Shadows
58. Fusion
59. Popcorn
60. Omelette
61. Birth
62. Maps
63. Chain
64. Plants
65. Coupling
66. Paint
67. Mickey Mouse
68. Words
69. Penetration
70. Eyes
71. Ego
72. Game
73. Umbrella
74. Mathematics
75. Joke
76. Maze
77. Slogan
78. X-Ray
79. Glue
80. Knots
81. Clouds
82. Body Parts
83. Rainbows
84. Machines
85. Clusters
86. Time
87. Bionics
88. Bug
89. Banners
90. Eating
91. Buildings
92. Torn Paper
93. Diary
94. Movie Hero
95. Destruction
96. Birdcage
97. Poetry
98. Anti-Gravity
99. Envelopes
100. Tower

**197. The Liberator** by René Magritte, 1947, 39" x 31" (99 x 78.7 cm), oil on canvas. Courtesy Los Angeles County Museum of Art, gift of William Copley. The perplexing quality of Magritte's images defy symbolic analysis. The title suggests that images are "liberated" from the conventions of symbolic communication.

*Irrational thoughts should be followed logically.* Sol LeWitt

## 6-4 / Neo-Dada

**Concept:** Making a collage from diverse images.

**Do:** 1. Cut images from magazines or newspapers, photocopy or photograph engravings from archival books or old dictionaries.

2. Combine them by carefully cutting and pasting to create a collage.

## 6-5 / Real-Life Surrealism

**Concept:** Narrating bizarre personal experiences or observations.

**Do:** 1. Write out a story of a real-life event or personal experience (either your own or one you have heard about) that you perceive as surreal.

2. Write out a story from a dream you have had that you perceive as bizarre or surreal.

3. Graphically illustrate the stories using an art medium of your choice.

## 6-6 / Anatomical Landscapes

**Concept:** Creating perspective drawings that include fragments of human anatomy.

**Do:** 1. Create a mixed-media composition involving collage and drawing. From magazines, cut out images of eyes or other anatomical parts and paste them down within a one- or two-point perspective drawing.

2. Select a variety of image sizes to place within the drawing, in accordance to the demands of perspective rendering.

## 6-7 / Three-Dimensional Surrealism

**Concept:** Creating a surreal portrait.

**Do:** 1. Get a styrofoam wig head (used as a wig stand) from a department store (or wad and tape newspapers into the form of a human head)

2. Transform it: add cloth, leather, buttons, rope, mechanical gadgets, bottle caps, wool, hat, paint, et cetera.

**above: 198. Defence Train** by Nicholas Roukes, 1980, collage.

**left: 199. Head** by Bob Thomas, 1980, mixed media. Courtesy the artist.

## 6-8 / Tribute to a Bizarre Event

**Concept:** Creating a surreal monument.

**Do:** 1. Make up an imaginary event that would rival a performance in *The Guinness Book of Records,* or choose an actual record from the book itself.

2. Create a trophy, monument, shrine, headstone, medal, or banner that recognizes and pays tribute to the meritorious achievement.

## 6-9 / Photocopies from Found Objects

**Concept:** Making black-and-white prints from materials arranged on a photocopying machine.

**Do:** 1. Make a collection of interesting found objects — watch parts, keys, tickets, household objects, photographs, tickets, string and so on.

2. Arrange the objects on the glass surface of the photocopying machine.

3. Make a print.

4. Color with felt pens.

## 6-10 / Survival Kit

**Concept:** Putting together a "save-the-species" kit.

**Do:** 1. Design a survival kit for one of the following endangered species:

- The Arctic Wolf
- The Canada Goose
- The Sea Turtle
- The Whooping Crane
- The Rhinoceros
- The Great White Whale
- The Bald Eagle
- The Student of the 80's
- Man of the Future

2. Use clear plastic (polyethylene) or cloth to create a bag. Within the bag, include all pertinent maps, special devices, instructions, tablets, pills, and "survival gear."

3. Label the kit appropriately.

**200. Intercontinental Art Troops Capture the Fur Lined Tea Cup** by Raphael Gomez, 1980, mixed media. Courtesy the artist.

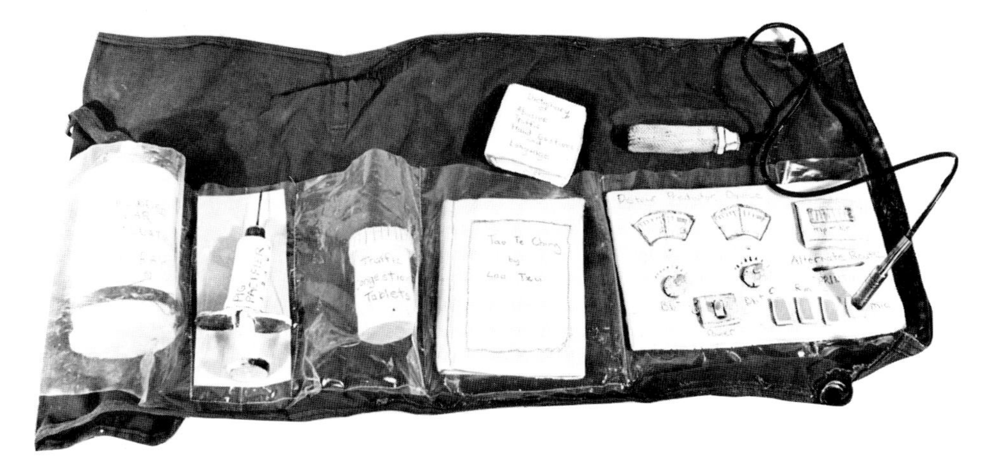


**201. Motorists' Survival Kit** by Drew Scott, 1981, 18" x 24" (45.7 x 60.9 cm), ceramic, cloth. Courtesy the artist.

right: 202. **Image Lift Collage** by Dan Metz, 1980, mixed media. Courtesy the artist.

## 6-11 / Image Lift Surrealism

**Concept:** Creating decals and image transfers for collage designs.

**Do:** 1. Cut out illustrations and photographic images from magazines.

2. Transfer the illustrations to a stretched and primed canvas in the following manner: (a) Brush acrylic medium on the surface of the illustrations, then press the images face down on the canvas. (b) Allow to dry thoroughly, then use a moist sponge to remove backing paper. The images will be transparent and reversed. Acrylic paint or gesso can also be used to make the transfers. Dampen paper before transfering to avoid air bubbles.

3. Use a free brush or hard-edge (masking tape) technique to heighten effects and unify the composition. Use thin washes of acrylic color (glazes) over some of the images, along with solid color painting, scumbling, and color texturing.

## 6-12 / Maze

**Concept:** Creating graphic labyrinths.

Labyrinths and mazes are designs involving intricate channels and blind alleys. Graphic mazes are a type of puzzle wherein participants seek to find their way from point "A" to point "Z" through a perplexing series of passageways and one-way corridors.

**Do:** 1. Draw a maze. Sketch out the preliminary drawing with pencil.

2. Make the final rendering in pen and ink on paper with a felt marker or an ink pen. Indicate the entrance to the maze with an arrow.

*Other maze-making activities:* (a) Glue cardboard or wood strips on a wood panel to construct a bas-relief maze. (b) Create a pin-ball game based on a maze design.

## 6-13 / X-Ray Image

**Concept:** Portraying images and their "inner workings."

**Do:** 1. Select photographic images such as heads, figures, machines, and buildings from magazines, newspapers, or posters.

2. Cut out a section of the images to suggest an "X-ray window."

3. Paste white drawing paper in back of the cut-out. Use your wildest thoughts to portray the "inner workings" of the subject. Combine pen and ink, collage, or any mixed media of your choice.

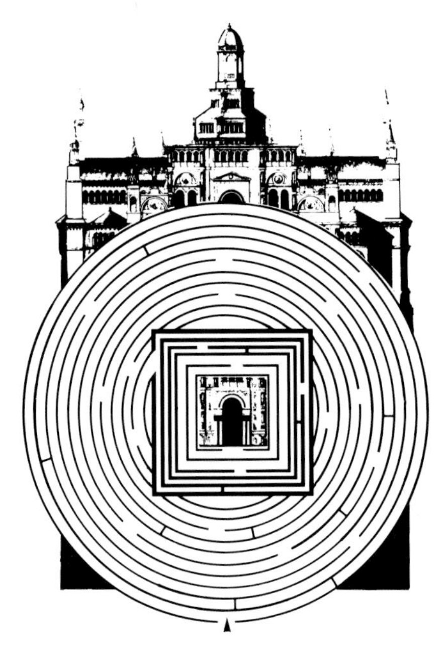

203. **Maze** by Stella Gordon, 1980, pen and ink drawing. Courtesy the artist.

## 6-14 / Color Photocopies from Collages

**Concept:** Exploring color photocopying processes as an art medium.

Color photocopying is a dye-transfer color reproduction process. Three process-color dyes — red, yellow, and blue — are coated on a continuous roll of aluminum foil. As the image is exposed, the appropriate filter determines the amount of each color in each area. These respective quantities are then transferred to the surface of the copy from the foil color sources.

An advantage of this process is its ability to change the color of the copies. Color settings can be adjusted so that, for example, the blue will not print. Thus, a full-color original can be reproduced in only red and yellow. By controlling the color setting, color copies can also be made from black-and-white originals. In contrast to traditional prints, each operation can be as individual as a separate drawing. The industry has made great improvements in this process and the color is permanent — except for direct sunlight, as with most artwork. —Tyler James Hoare

**Do:** 1. Make a collage: cut out different images from magazines and posters.

2. Carefully combine and paste the images to a sheet of construction paper. Add elements of drawing.

3. Use a color photocopying machine to make prints from the collage.

**above right: 204. McCal** by Tyler James Hoare, 1975, 20-1/2" x 20-/12" (52 x 52 cm), color photocopy on wood. Using a 3M® color photocopy machine, the artist made eight prints from a 35mm slide. (The slide is reversed to make four prints.) Segments of the prints are pasted together to create a kaleidoscopic pattern.

## 6-15 /. Estranged Object

**Concept:** Decorating a three-dimensional object with drawings that are completely irrelevant to its shape or function.

**Do:** 1. Select a commonplace object such as a bottle, clock, baseball bat, or any other three-dimensional object. (Casts from the human body or store mannequin parts are also useful subjects).

2. Prime the surface of the object with white acrylic gesso (two coats, sanding between coats).

3. Paint a design on the three-dimensional surface that is completely irrelevant to its shape: clouds, landscapes, poetry, rainbows, a street scene.

**205. Iron** by Michael Peabody, 1980, mixed media. Courtesy the artist.

## 6-16 / Afterimage

**Concept:** Orientation and experimentation with afterimage effects.

**Do:** 1. Research various forms of afterimage phenomena. For example: colored shapes produce complementary colors as afterimages; black dots create illusive white dots as afterimages; dissimilar shapes may be amalgamated through afterimage projection (bird-in-the-cage phenomena), and so forth.

2. Create an art form that makes use of afterimage phenomena.

## 6-17/ Optical Illusions

**Concept:** Using optical illusions in art.

**Do:** 1. Examine the optical illusions on page 124 carefully.

2. Select one of the figures and use it as a basis for creating a pen-and-ink drawing.

3. Think of other ways of using optical illusions in art.

**206. Picasso Cups** by Jasper Johns, 1972, 22" x 32" (56 x 81.2 cm), lithograph. Courtesy Leo Castelli Gallery, New York.

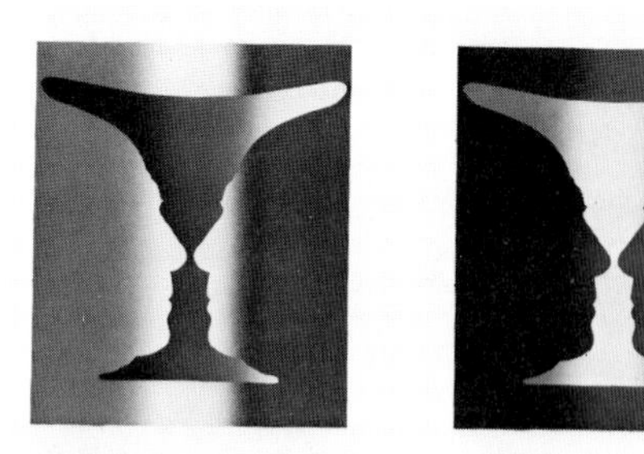

**207. Afterimage Phenomena.** Stare at the bird for one minute. Then look at the cage. The bird will mysteriously appear inside the cage.

## 6-18 / Strobe Art

**Concept:** Creating optical-illusion art that combines graphic design, movement, and strobe lighting.

**Do:** 1. Cut out a 12" (30.5 cm) circle from cardboard or illustration board.

2. Draw a series of concentric circles, 1" to 2" (2.5 to 5 cm) apart, with the disk.

3. Use acrylic paints to create designs within the segments of the disk.

4. Mount the disk on the shaft of a motor that is secured to a table. Use a dimmer switch to control the speed of the motor.

5. Illuminate the disk with a strobe lamp in a darkened room. Vary the speed of the motor to produce different effects. You will note that the shapes within the concentric circles will simultaneously appear to move at different speeds; some will appear to stop, while others will appear to reverse their motion. (Disks painted with fluorescent paints can be illuminated with black-light strobes for dramatic effects.)

## 6-19 / Kaleidoscopic Construction

**Concept:** Experimenting with the combination of virtual (reflected) images and three-dimensional shapes.

**Do:** 1. Get three 12" (30.5 cm) square mirror panels and tape them together to form a "corner" (see illustration).

2. Cut designed shapes from wood, plastic, cardboard, and other materials. Arrange them on the surface of the mirror. (Note that the designs "complete themselves" through their reflection; for example, a half circle becomes a full circle.)

3. Attach the components to the mirror surface with a glue that will stick to glass.

above: **208. Strobe Wheel** by Nicholas Roukes, 1980, 28" diameter (71.1 cm), acrylic.

## 6-20 / Moiré

**Concept:** Using moiré patterns in art.

Moiré is a visual effect caused whenever two repetitive structures are superimposed with elements almost congruent, or whenever two families of linear patterns are overlayed, causing lines to cross at small angles. The resultant interference effects are called moiré patterns and are commonly observed in overlapping silk patterns, parallel fence patterns, or doubled screens.

**Do:** 1. With pen and ink, create a design composed of closely spaced lines, dots, or shapes.

2. Make two duplicates of the design on transparent film. (Original designs may be photocopied, or designs may be drawn directly on clear plastic surfaces with appropriate ink pens.)

3. Attach the designs to both sides of a shallow wooden frame. (Determine the thickness of the frame by trial and error.)

**209. Symmetric Illusion** by Norman Dillsman, 1980, 12" x 12" x 12" (30.5 x 30.5 x 30.5 cm). Courtesy the artist.

## 6-21 / Cryptic Images

**Concept:** Creating a drawing that contains hidden images within its composition.

**Do:** 1. Select an image to act as the principal subject for this drawing.

2. Try to cleverly implant cryptic images within the composition.

3. Make a preliminary sketch in pencil. Render the final drawing with pen and ink.

## 6-22 / Fantasy Card

**Concept:** Expressing a fantasy theme through symmetrical design.

**Do:** 1. Create a fantasy version of a playing card such as the king, queen, or jack.

2. Use any subject of your choice as a basis for making a portrait.

3. Work on a large sheet of paper, 18" x 24" (45.7 x 61 cm) in size, and draw only half of the design (head and torso).

4. Trace to illustration paper. Make a reverse drawing and trace to the lower portion of the design to complete the composition.

5. Render with poster paints or acrylics.

**above left: 210. The King of the Beasts** by Raffaello Dvorak, 1980, 25" x 36" (63.5 x 91.4 cm), drawing. Courtesy the artist. The artist challenges the viewer to discover the myriad animal forms cryptically implanted within the drawing.

**above right: 211. Fantasy Card** by Tim Klaxman, 1980, tempera. Courtesy the artist.

**below: 212. Electriclawnmowingiron** by Paul De Nooijer, 1977, photograph. Courtesy the artist.

**213. The Choir** by Leslie Jean Goldberg, 1973, 3'6'' x 2' x 2' (106.7 x 61 x 61 cm), bleached muslin, unspun hair, watercolors, tape player. Courtesy The Museum of Contemporary Crafts, New York. A sound track of choral music is incorporated within this whimsical sculpture.

## 6-23 / Acoustic Construction

**Concept:** Creating a three-dimensional sculpture that incorporates sound.

**Do:** 1. Select a theme.

2. Use either rigid or soft materials to make a three-dimensional structure.

3. Incorporate some type of sound-producing mechanism, device, or tape player within the base or interior structure of the sculpture.

## 6-24 / Surreal Tableau

**Concept:** Composing and photographing a surreal three-dimensional tableau. According to Webster's dictionary, Surrealism is defined as the practice of producing fantastic or incongruous imagery and effects in art, literature, or theatre by means of unnatural juxtapositions and combinations.

**Do:** 1. Select objects, props, costumes, participants, an environment and compose a surrealistic three-dimensional composition.

2. Photograph the result.

**214. Image Duplicator** by Roy Lichtenstein, 1963, 24" x 20" (61 x 50.8 cm), acrylic on canvas. Courtesy Leo Castelli Gallery, New York.

## 6-25 / Art from Comics

**Concept:** Using comic strips as a basis for design experiments.

**Do:** 1. Cut out a single frame from a comic strip.

2. Enlarge the design to at least 20" x 20" (50.8 x 50.8 cm).

3. Change color or text from the original in your rendering.

4. Render with tempera or acrylics.

# GLOSSARY

**Afterimage.** A visual sensation or image that is sustained after its external cause has been removed.

**Analogy.** An inferred relationship between things that are otherwise unlike. Likenesses may be drawn on structural, intellectual, or psychological levels.

**Anamorphic.** Anamorphic drawings or paintings are distorted images that are corrected when viewed in an anamorphic mirror — usually a cylinder-shaped mirror placed perpendicularly to the image.

**Anomaly.** Deviation from common rules; an abnormal presentation; situations that refuse to correspond to existing standards.

**Bas-relief.** A form of sculpture wherein elements project into space from a background or ground plane. *Basso Rilievo* (bas-relief), or low relief, indicates forms having a small amount of projection, as opposed to high relief forms, which jut out radically from the ground plane.

**Chance.** A random, accidental, or spontaneous manner of working, which may use dice, spinners, or automatic means of initiating or controlling the development of an art form.

**Ciphers.** A composition of symbolic letters to form a secret message system.

**Closure.** The ability to mentally complete a partially complete image.

**Code.** A set of symbols used to form a communication system.

**Collage.** A pictorial technique involving the use of decorative papers, photographic images, designs on two-dimensional surfaces, and so on, which are cut or torn and subsequently arranged and pasted on a suitable surface.

**Concept.** A "pivotal idea" implying mental polarization of thought toward a particular purpose. A concept may also be thought of as a "focusing lens" or "funnel" for the intellect and imagination to integrate experiences, knowledge, and experimentation.

**Conceptual art.** Conceptual art has been construed to mean investigations and presentations of information structures, inquiry into relationships between events and conceptions. Conceptual art is of a non-object, non-object-making, and non-art-aesthetic modality, usually presented in the form of charts and documentation, such as visual images with supporting text. Presentations often deal with "re-definitions of art", art-language systems, and syntactics.

**Cyborg.** A human being linked to mechanical devices for purposes of survival in a hostile environment.

**Dada.** A movement of social revolt among European artists during the First World War. Absurd, bizarre, and nonsense activities were passed off as "art," intending to shock public complacency. The destructive, non-art qualities of Dada gave rise to schools of assemblage art, Surrealism, and subjectively oriented art forms.

**Déjà vu.** The perception of an experience as one that has "already happened before."

**Eidetic.** Having photographic-like memory; a memory of a highly vivid and detailed nature.

**Empathy.** Projecting personal or subjective states to another person or object; evoking a capacity to identify emotionally with another person, or to infuse a subjective quality into an inanimate object.

**Encoding.** Transforming information from one state to another. The transference of personal experience and knowledge to abstract graphic forms and symbols.

**Equivocal.** Images that may be perceived or interpreted in more than one way; "flip-flop" optical illusions, multiple ideas or images, and so forth.

**Homeostasis.** A stable state or equilibrium, or a tendency toward such a state; a means of keeping things in a balanced state.

**Hybrid.** A strange offspring produced by the amalgamation or mating of two diverse breeds, either in animals, races, objects, ideas, or elements.

**Imaging.** The production of mental images. Memory images are retrieved from past experiences; imaginary images are reconstructions of past experiences rearranged by creative fantasy.

**Labyrinth.** A structure involving intricate passageways and blind alleys; a perplexing path from one point to another; a confusing or mazelike structure.

**Metamorphosis.** An evolution or change from one form or state to another.

**Metaphor.** A figure of speech or visual presentation in which a word, phrase, or image is used in place of another to suggest a likeness between them, while in the process formulating a new concept for the imagination.

**Moiré.** A visual effect, oscillating in nature, that is created whenever two repetitive structures are superimposed with elements that are almost congruent, or whenever two families of lines cross at small angles. (Noticeable in doubled screens, fences, and silk patterns.)

**Mnemonic.** A device or code used to aid or improve the memory.

**Myths.** Although commonly thought of as "false stories," myths are also truths presented in irrational forms. Tales and stories are narrated, acted out, or pictorialized to reflect the reality of a culture; its values, ideas, truths, fears, dreams, and superstitions are codified within the structure of the myth.

**Onomatopoeia.** The naming of an action or object by the similarity of a sound pattern to its function or quality.

**Paradox.** A seemingly contradictory statement, situation, or image that defies logical comprehension.

**Performance art.** "Live art" or action art. The creation of an art form requiring interdisciplinary media, settings, and performers.

**Photomontage.** A collage method involving only photographic images, which are cut and pieced together.

**Ready-mades.** Commonplace objects found in basements, attics, flea markets, or junkyards that can be utilized or incorporated into art forms.

**Ritual.** Ceremonious action or behavior that is predetermined and designated to be "acted out."

**Score.** A written or graphic plan or guide for realizing any kind of creative work. Examples: music or dance notation, drama script, or directions for performance pieces.

**Serendipity.** Fortuitous discovery by chance or accident; controlled "chance happenings". Works of art are often initiated without prior visualization. The artist's will to set up situations wherein reciprocating actions between the artist and his medium can be initiated are called serendipitous. Once started, this action is used to bring about symbolic content and structure through the give-and-take process of creative manipulation.

**Subconscious.** Existing in the mind, but below the level of conscious awareness.

**Subjective.** Qualities or states of mind that evoke personal, emotional, or introspective imagery. The absence of objective reality.

**Subliminal Stimulation.** Communication directed to subconscious levels of awareness.

**Surreal.** Incredible images or situations that challenge our concepts of reality. Bizarre or illogical situations having the irrationality of dream states; the apprehension of fantastic imagery created by unnatural juxtapositions or the destruction of laws of nature or logic.

**Symbols.** Codes, patterns, and visual configurations that represent reality in abstract terms.

**Synaesthetic.** Simultaneous sensory perception and/or reversed sensory perception, for example, "hearing colors," "seeing sounds."

**Synectic.** The synthesis of disparities; producing unified or cohesive structures and ideas from seemingly incompatible elements.

**Syntactics.** Arranging together. Dealing with relationships of abstract signs or expressions and their signification or interpretation.

**Tableau.** An art form involving components that are arranged on a tablelike setting. A stagelike arrangement of elements within a miniature environment.

**Utopia.** An imaginary place of ideal perfection.

**Virtual form.** The image of something, but not the substance, as in the reflected images of mirrors, or those produced by natural phenomena (rainbows, and the like).

# BIBLIOGRAPHY


Arguelles, José A. *The Transformative Vision.* Berkeley, Ca. Chambahala. 1975.

Arnheim, Rudolf. *Visual Thinking.* Berkeley, Ca. University of California Press. 1971.

Borges, Jorge Luis. *The Book of Imaginary Beings.* Middlesex, England. Penguin Books. 1969.

Burland, C.A. *Myths of Life and Death.* London. MacMillan. 1974.

d'Arbeloff, Natalie. *Designing With Natural Forms.* London. B.T. Batsford. 1973.

DeBono, Edward. *Lateral Thinking.* London. Ward Lock Education Ltd. 1970.

Ehrenzweig, Anton. *The Hidden Order of Art.* London. Weidenfeld and Nicolson. 1967.

Eliot, Alexander. *Myths.* New York. McGraw-Hill Book Co. 1976.

Gablik, Suzi. *Magritte.* London. Thames and Hudson. 1970.

Goldberg, Rosalee. *Performance: Live Art 1909 to the Present.* New York. Abrams. 1978.

Gombrich, E.H. *Art and Illusion.* London. Phaidon. 1972.

Gordon, J.J. *Synectics.* New York. Harper and Row. 1961.

Gregory, R.L. *The Intelligent Eye.* London. Weidenfeld and Nicolson. 1970.

Grunfeld, F.V. *Games of the World: How to Make Them, How to Play Them, How They Came to Be.* New York. Ballantine Books. 1977.

Haeckel, Ernst. *Art Forms in Nature.* New York. Dover Publications. 1974.

Hammacher, A.M. *Magritte.* New York. Abrams. 1977.

Ions, Veronica. *The World's Mythology.* London. Hamlyn. 1974.

Janis, Harriet; Blesh, Rudi. *Collage.* New York. Chilton. 1962.

Jung, Carl. *Man and His Symbols.* New York. Doubleday and Co. 1964.

Kepes, Gyorgy (editor). *Sign, Image, Symbol.* New York. George Braziller. 1966.

Kirk, G.S. *Myth.* Berkeley, Ca. University of California Press. 1973.

Koch, Rudolf. *The Book of Signs.* New York. Dover Publications. 1955.

Kostelanetz, Richard. *The Theatre of Mixed Means.* London. Pitman. 1970.

Langer, Suzanne. *Feeling and Form.* New York. Charles Scribner's Sons. 1953.

Locher, J.L. (editor). *The World of M.C. Escher.* New York. Abrams. 1971.

Love, B. *Play the Game: The Book You Can Play.* London. Michael Joseph Publication. 1978.

Matthews, J.H. *The Imagery of Surrealism.* Syracuse, New York. Syracuse University Press. 1977.

Maue, Kenneth. *Water in the Lake: Real Events for the Imagination.* New York. Harper and Row. 1979.

Ornstein, Robert. *The Psychology of Consciousness.* San Francisco. W.H. Freeman. 1972.

Osborn, Alex. *Applied Imagination.* New York. Charles Scribner's Sons. 1963.

Pavey, Don. *Art-Based Games.* London. Methuen. 1979.

Samuels, Nancy and Mike. *Seeing with the Mind's eye.* New York. Random House. 1975.

Schwenk, Theodor. *Sensitive Chaos: The Creation of Flowing Forms in Water and Air.* London. Rudolf Steiner. 1965.

Seitz, William C. *The Art of Assemblage.* New York. Museum of Modern Art. 1961.

Stevens, Peter S. *Patterns in Nature.* Boston. Little, Brown and Co. 1974.

Thompson D'Arcy. *On Growth and Form.* London. Cambridge University Press. 1961.

Waldberg, Patrick. *Surrealism.* London. Thames and Hudson. 1965.

Whyte, Lancelot Law. *Aspects of Form.* London. Percy Lund, Humphries and Co. 1968.

# Index

# ABOUT THE AUTHOR:

NICHOLAS ROUKES has written numerous articles and books on art. His paintings and sculptures have been shown at the San Francisco Museum of Art, the Stanford Art Gallery, The Stanford Research Institute, the Phoenix Art Gallery, and the Bolles Gallery in San Francisco, among other galleries both in the United States and Canada.

Roukes, professor of art and art education at the University of Calgary (Canada), has for over 20 years been investigating new approaches and techniques for the fine arts. He is author of *Sculpture in Plastics* and *Masters of Wood Sculpture,* both published by Watson-Guptill Publications of New York.

# Notes

# Notes